PHILOSOPHY FOR TEENS

Ideas and Ideals

By

Joseph A. Grispino

Tucson, Arizona

Third Millennium Publishing
**A Cooperative of Writers and Resources
On the INTERNET at 3mpub.com**
http://3mpub.com

ISBN 1-932657-38-X

290 pages

© 2005 by Joseph A. Grispino

All rights reserved under International and Pan-American Copyright Conventions. Published in the United States of America by Third Millennium Publishing, located on the INTERNET at http://3mpub.com.

Third Millennium Publishing
1931 East Libra Drive
Tempe, AZ 85283
mccollum@3mpub.com

CONTENTS

PREFACE VII
ACKNOWLEDGMENTS XI
INTRODUCTION 1
   CHAPTER 1 3
      There Are Only Three Royal Highways To The Kingdom Of Knowledge
   CHAPTER 2 11
      Application Of The Three Ways Of Knowing To ESP
   CHAPTER 3 15
      Introducing The Prima Donnas: A Theologian, A Philosopher, Miss Ethics
LOGIC 29
   CHAPTER 4 31
      Are Science And Religion Still Boxing? The Scopes Trial
   CHAPTER 5 39
      I'm Too Young To Think Logically
   CHAPTER 6 49
      Superstitions But Fallacies? Superstitions? Me?
INTERLUDE 59
   CHAPTER 7 61
      The Media: Are Journalists Ethical? Trust Them? How Much?
   CHAPTER 8 69
      Who Am I? Something? (Matter) Or Somebody? (Matter-Spirit)
   CHAPTER 9 73
      Where Am I? Was There Always A Universe?
   CHAPTER 10 77
      Will There Always Be A Universe? Candide By Voltaire
   CHAPTER 11 83
      Can I Prove That God Exists? Why So Much Evil?
   CHAPTER 12 93
      What Is The Best Type Of Government And For Whom? Monarchy, Dictatorship, Democracy. Socialists vs. Capitalists

ETHICAL WARM-UP 105

Chapter 13 107
May I Go On A Civil Disobedience Spree?

Chapter 14 109
Can I Be A Patriot And A Cosmopolitan Citizen?

Chapter 15 115
Why Can't Church And State Get Along?

Chapter 16 123
Has The State The Right To Inflict The Death Penalty? Debate Rules

Chapter 17 133
Is It Ethical To Punish Human Beings?

INTERLUDE 139

Chapter 18 141
What's A Happy Life? Can I Achieve It? The Happy Test

Chapter 19 147
There Can Only Be Three Types Of Friends

Chapter 20 153
There Are Only Three Reasons Why People Laugh

ETHICS 157

Chapter 21 159
How Am I Expected To Know The Difference Between Right And Wrong? A Religious Ethical Style, A Philosophical Ethical Style, An Ethics Test

Chapter 22 169
A Chart Of Lies: A Way Of Life? Or Be Myself?

MID-TERM SELF-EXAMINATION 175

Chapter 23 177
In Which Of The Six States Of Moral Development Am I?

ETHICAL ISSUES 181

Chapter 24 183
Gambling: Crime? Entertainment?

Chapter 25 193
What's Pornography? What's Beauty?

CHAPTER 26..201
    Is Adolescent Sex Moral?

CHAPTER 27..207
    The Rights Of Gays/Lesbians

CHAPTER 28..213
    What's All This Shouting About Abortion?

CHAPTER 29..219
    Do Animals Have Rights?

CHAPTER 30..227
    What's All This Weeping About Euthanasia?

EPILOGUE..231
    What's The Biggest Defect Of The Human Race?

APPENDICES, NOTES AND BIBLIOGRAPHY 239

APPENDIX A..241
    One Liner Meditations On Seneca's Ethical Tunes

APPENDIX B..245
    Chapters According To Their Literary Forms

APPENDIX C..246
    Suggested Teachers For Friendly Chapters

APPENDIX D..247
    How To Use This Book And An Explanation Of The Chapter Arrangement In The Table Of Contents

BOOK NOTES 250
SELECTED BIBLIOGRAPHY 258
ABOUT THE AUTHOR 275
BOOK INDEX 277

PREFACE

How will high school graduates defend themselves from the sharks of deception lurking in the alleyways of life? Sharks like advertisers when they create desires for things we don't need; businesspersons when they hope our eyes won't fall on the fine print; reporters when they slant the news on TV, radio, newspapers, magazines; politicians when they represent lobbyists instead of needy citizens.

These wicked thoughts rumbled in my head after I retired from teaching philosophy to college students. Leisure allowed me to reflect about the few years I had taught Latin to high school students. Concern obsessed me about high school graduates who will never attend college and college students who will never enroll in a philosophy course.

By philosophy I mean practical philosophy with an emphasis on logic and ethics.

The Sword of Logic

Years in the arena of the classroom and in the arena of public life convinced me that cloudy thinking, even in educated minds, seeps down from the failure of differentiating scientific, philosophical, and religious problems. This master persuasion did not germinate from the soil of logic textbooks. Therefore I have insisted on how to recognize these three sets of problems in several chapters.

The Shield of Ethics

Chapter 21 unfolds a few practical guidelines on how to judge right and wrong actions regardless of one's religion or the lack thereof. (Chapter 23 outlines six stages of moral development.) These ethical guidelines are applicable in all the chapters featuring the ethical issues of the death penalty, pornography, abortion, etc.

A vein of tolerance urges its path throughout all the ethical disputes. Tolerance is a virtue by which a person strives to understand and to allow another person's different view. America is the only country in the world that is home to such a large population of different peoples with so many different religions. It remains an ongoing experiment whether we can all live in peace in spite of our various religious beliefs and practices.

Let's Be Practical

This book skips over the history of philosophy and speculative problems such as free will and whether we can prove that the watermelon is on the table and not in our head. None of the practical issues selected dies from exhausted treatment. I selected practical problems that will last the lifetime of high school students. As in literary anthologies, it is impossible that the selections will please everyone. Technical words are avoided like the plague or immediately explained. The vocabulary is designed to express not to impress.

The purpose of the book is to equip the reader with a method of approaching problems: to locate the precise problem, to select the appropriate thinking tools with which to analyze and discuss, to avoid the obvious incorrect answers, to separate the pro and con answers, to find the direction leading to the correct answer, and sometimes to find the exact answer.

The False Fear of Philosophy

If it's true that many admirable Christians run the other way when they see a philosopher, to them I say there is no confrontation between philosophy and religion. Some rowdy philosophers in past history gave philosophy a bad name. Forgive them.

From the infant centuries of the Christian religion to the present time, philosophy served as the handmaiden of religion. Philosophy was always ready to show the reasonableness of religious teachings. A lyrical axiom always floated in clerical circles: the better philosopher you are, the better theologian you will be.

To be different is not the same as to confront. This book donates a generous amount of space to illustrate the important distinction between the two disciplines. Philosophy, properly understood, will not weaken one's religion but strengthen it.

If this book shapes the lifestyle for good of only one student, it would have been worth the toil.

ACKNOWLEDGMENTS

I am profoundly indebted to my wife, Phyllis Johansen Cook, for her insightful editorial contributions and to Jean Walsh for her devoted computer expertise.

Many thoughts expressed in this book can be traced to the numerous 101 philosophy textbooks used in my courses over the past decades. To their authors I acknowledge a deep gratitude. Their names are legion.

INTRODUCTION

CHAPTER 1

There Are Only Three Royal Highways To The Kingdom Of Knowledge

"A good mind possesses a kingdom." (1)

Seneca

The Kingdom Of Knowledge

Scientist	Philosopher	Non-Specialist	Mystic
I like senses	I like reason	I like authority	I like intuition

Announcement

Everything we humans know flows from our senses, reason, authority. These are the only three highways to knowledge simply because of the structure of the universe and of ourselves.

John Doe: Why must we be aware of these three separate tools of collecting knowledge?

Philosopher: Awareness will help us to think more clearly.

Scientist: And assist us in avoiding unending discussions. Excuse me. I must return to my laboratory.

The Five Senses

When Mary observes, "It's raining," her sense of sight is working. When Cindy remarks, "It's noisy," her sense of hearing is operating. When Nathan shouts, "What a delicious banana!" his sense of taste is active. When Keith whispers, "This rose is fragrant," his sense of smell is engaged. "What a soft marshmallow," signifies that Angela is utilizing her sense of touch.

Scientists

Scientists specialize in harnessing the senses to harvest an abundance of facts. When these dedicated workers are absorbed in experiments, they press into service an arsenal of instruments, which extend the powers of the senses. The microscope stretches the power of sight. Scientists are fond of the term, "empirical evidence," evidence gathered by the five senses as in the examples above. Naturally, they also use reason and the authority of earlier scientists.

Reason

Just as scientists emphasize senses, philosophers emphasize reason. When Shawn jogged by the smoldering embers of the local bank, his reason invited him to conclude, "A fire burned down this building." What caused Shawn to arrive at this conclusion? After all, he did not witness the fire. Apparently, the empirical evidence, the embers, impacted his senses of sight and smell causing his reason to conclude that a fire burned the bank. From one source of knowledge, the senses, Shawn continued to another source of knowledge, reason.

A celebrated example of reasoning after the use of the senses is that of Darwin, the English biologist, who saw thousands of animals and fossil remains, i.e., empirical evidence, which guided him to reason to the theory, not the fact, of evolution. This is an example of the process of reasoning without specifying whether it's correct or incorrect reasoning.

Philosophers

Philosophers enjoy a reputation as thinkers; scientists as doers. Before philosophers begin to puzzle over a problem related to science they peep into the laboratories of the scientists to learn from them. Afterwards philosophers ask questions which lie beyond the range of scientific inquiry. For example, philosophers learn the big-bang theory and then ask themselves, "Was there always matter before the big-bang? Will matter always exist?" (Chaps. 9 and 10 explore these questions.)

A scientist does not fuss over such inquiries; he lacks empirical evidence. A philosopher jumps into these inquiries precisely because there is no empirical evidence.

If we glance at scientists and philosophers, we notice that they both sport the same t-shirt with the words, "Show me. I come from Missouri." They are informing us that they demand empirical evidence and reasons respectively.

Incidentally, philosophers and mathematicians, from masters of arithmetic to trigonometry, must be blood brothers because both shun authority as much as their specialties allow.

Authority

The third royal highway to the kingdom of knowledge is authority: statements of experts of various specialties. Our brains are overheated with facts accepted on the authority of parents, teachers, doctors, scientists, historians, etc. At some future date, a cultural anthropologist may calculate the average daily frequency that we humans utilize empirical evidence, authority, and reason.

Non-Specialists

We are all non-specialists in the areas of knowledge about which we know little or nothing. Therefore, we are compelled to depend on experts. Due to our limitation of time and ability we accept the authority of others for tons of knowledge. Up to the age of reason we rely on the authority of our elders. This dependency continues into adulthood. Who can deny that our knowledge of history is almost entirely grounded on the authority of historians? We never saw Julius Caesar invade Britain but we believe historians who "prove" he did.

Mystics and Their Intuitions

Does anyone travel on the fourth highway to the kingdom of knowledge called intuition? (Dictionaries list various meanings of intuition.) Religious mystics, (Meister Eckhart, St. Theresa of Avila) and non-religious, (Alfred Lord Tennyson) assassins of kings and presidents all claim to be regular hikers on the mystic road less traveled. Their source of knowledge is not senses, reason or authority, but a direct line to God or the Ultimate. Is this direct line a trustworthy fountain of knowledge?

"Yes" thunder the mystics. So firmly do they believe in God's communications to them personally that they are willing to be burned at the stake.

"No" counter their objectors. "Or at least prove it! With all due respect, you may be suffering from hallucinations, even saintly ones."

Summary

The only tools we humans use to learn anything are the senses, reason, and authority. The scientists rely heavily on the senses for their accumulation of knowledge; the philosophers on reason; and the non-specialists on authority of experts.

Working Out

1. Write in between the parentheses to indicate which of the three sources of knowledge the statement is based on: senses, reason, authority.

    a) The date of Napoleon's retreat from Russia is 1812 according to my history book. (   )

    b) Adrian whispers to Simon: "As soon as I entered my room and viewed the wreckage (   ), I knew that a thug had burglarized my apartment." (   )

2. Scribble three sentences exemplifying the use of the senses, three exemplifying the use of reason, and three the use of authority.

3. Are there intelligent human beings besides us earthlings in the universe?

Which ONE of the three responses would you choose and explain why.

a) Yes, God told me in a dream last night. (Appeal to intuition)

b) Yes, some scientists say so. (Appeal to authority)

c) No, not until you show me one. (Appeal to senses)

4. Although there is nothing in fictional literature to illustrate the three sources of knowledge as expressed in this chapter, there is a fascinating "Benjy section" of Faulkner's novel, The Sound and The Fury, in which all the events are narrated through the eyes of a 33-year-old idiot. The events are sensory, without order or logic. On the other hand, the "Quentin section" is narrated by a reasoning, intelligent, suicidal mind. Contrast the two types of thinking (the sensory and the reasoning) with examples from the novel.

5. Comment on the epigraph.

A Richter Scale of Truth

"The most important solutions in life are usually those of probability."

F. S. de Laplace

I got FACTS I got OPINIONS I got GUESSES I got (plenty of) NOTHING

Two of the royal highways to the kingdom of knowledge are the senses and reason. Might it be useful to become aware of an evaluation of statements based on the senses and reason according to the state of mind regarding truth? A Richter scale from certitude to ignorance may help. An awareness of evaluation of statements sharpens our analytic skills.

EVALUATION of statements	DEGREE of certitude	DESCRIPTION	EXAMPLE
Fact	10	Statement of certitude with empirical evidence	I see a cow.
Opinion	7	More probable statement with much evidence	He's guilty beyond a reasonable doubt.
Opinion	5	Less probable statement with little evidence	All nations will live in peace.
Guess (impressions, hunches)	1	Statement with no evidence, only feelings	The teacher does not like me.
Ignorance	0	Statement with no evidence, no feelings. Culpable ignorance	"Officer, I did not know the speed limit."
Ignorance	0	Inculpable ignorance	"I don't understand Einstein."

Climbing Exercises on the Richter Scale (2)

1. Construct a Richter Scale of your own or revamp the scale above. You might prefer to say that all nations will live in peace is a guess.

2. Substitute all the examples above with your own examples.

3. Comment on the epigraph.

CHAPTER 2

Application Of The Three Ways Of Knowing To ESP

"How can I know what I think till I see what I say?"

Graham Wallas

Since we collect knowledge through the senses, reason, and authority, we may well ask which of these three do the practitioners of extrasensory perception (ESP) use to collect their knowledge? ESP is also known as psychic phenomena, paranormal phenomena, parapsychology. Before answering the question let's look at four types of ESP.

CLAIRVOYANCE is the mental power of seeing objects, which are not present to the senses, e.g., guessing at cards.

TELEPATHY is the mental power of communicating with the brain of another person, dead or alive, by extrasensory means, e.g., without or beyond the normal use of the senses.

Notice that the clairvoyant claims that her information leaps out of an object whereas the telepathist claims that her information leaps out of a person.

Two cautionary steps are advisable before believing a clairvoyant or a telepathist. Step 1: Is there proof-positive that the practitioner had no knowledge whatsoever about the object or client prior to the session? Step 2: One should beware that a telepathist may formulate a general statement and the client may read details into it and attribute them to the telepathist. Once, a telepathist declared to a client that she would soon receive a visitor. The wide-eyed client exclaimed: "How did you know that my Nebraska friend whom I have not seen for a decade will visit me next week?"

PSYCHOKINESIS (PK or telekinesis) is the mental power of moving other people, animals, objects. Psychokinesis also includes levitation, bending objects, psychic healing, hypnotism.

It's time to answer the question: which of the three ways of knowing (senses, reason, authority) do the practitioners of ESP use?

ESP practitioners do not claim that their source of information is senses, reason or authority. Whether they are aware of it or not their information derives from the senses. How? Nobody knows. Could undetectable wavelengths travel between the practitioner's brain and that of the client? Could wavelengths travel between them after they each touch some common object like car keys? It's possible and perhaps probable. So far scientists have not detected such fine energy waves between practitioner and client.

Uri Geller, the so-called "world's greatest psychic" comes to mind but he has been repeatedly evaluated as a fraud. (1)

PRECOGNITION (foreknowledge) is the mental power of obtaining information from a future event in a dream, vision, intuition, that corresponds to an actual later event. For instance, Paul dreams that he will accidentally run his SUV over a little boy wearing green pants. The next morning while he is driving to his office he does exactly that. Paul believed that the future action (the accident) directly caused his present knowledge of the accident (in his dream) and caused the accident itself the next day.

Paul's precognition assumes a different notion of time. We commonly think of time as present, past, and future. On the contrary, precognition conceives present, past, and future time as all three eternally in the present time.

Paul's precognition assumes a different notion of cause and effect. We commonly think of a cause first and its effect afterwards. On the contrary precognition conceives the effect first (the accident) and its cause (the dream) afterwards.

In conclusion, precognition is false in the present world order. It may be true in another world order with a different notion of both time and the law of cause-effect. (2)

Exercises

1. How do predictions of war with a foreign country or predictions of the decline of the stock market differ from precognition?

2. Palmistry is "the art or practice of reading a person's character or aptitudes and especially his past and possible future from the general character and shape of his hands and fingers and lines, mounts, and marks on the palms-called also chirognomy, chiromancy," (Webster's dictionary). (3) Is this definition of palmistry an example of clairvoyance? Of telepathy? Give a reason for or against palmistry?

3. Graphology is "the study of handwriting especially for the purpose of character analysis," (Webster's dictionary). Why would you say that graphology, if true, is an example of clairvoyance? Give a reason for or

against graphology.

4. Physiognomy is "the technique or art of discovering temperament and character…from facial features, (it's) fortune telling . . . by reading a face . . ." (Webster's dictionary). Is physiognomy, if true, an example of clairvoyance, of telepathy or both? Give a reason for or against physiognomy.

5. A suggested gabfest: Share stories that you and your friends experienced which resemble the four types of ESP above. After each story critique its credibility.

CHAPTER 3

Introducing The Prima Donnas:
A Theologian, A Philosopher, Miss Ethics, Miss Bible

"Man is but a reed, the weakest in nature, but he is a thinking reed."

Pascal

FLASHBACK: Chap.1 sketched how all knowledge derives from the senses (emphasized by scientists), reason (emphasized by philosophers), and authority (emphasized by non-specialists).

FLASHFORWARD: Is there another source of knowledge called faith in a Bible, emphasized by religious believers and theologians, be they Christians, Jews, Muslims, etc.? The educated non-believer often hears believers assert that their Bible is a supernatural authority of knowledge. An American, tolerant of others' views, would want to understand how biblical believers think.

Theologian: Thank you. Just as you believe in the authority of a medical doctor as a spigot of natural knowledge, likewise we religious people believe in the authority of a Bible as a fountain of supernatural knowledge, e.g., the existence of heaven. Supernatural truths are not experienced through the senses nor grasped by reason nor accepted on the authority of any human being. They are accepted on the supernatural authority of God through a Bible.

Student Dan: Now that we studied four sources of knowledge: the senses, reason, natural authority, supernatural authority, let's move on and define religion.

Theologian: Theologians shake hands in agreement that there is no satisfactory definition of religion. They also agree that the best definition is a list of the ingredients of religion.

Philosopher: By the by, since the philosophers also agree that there is no satisfactory definition of philosophy, let's explain the difference between religion and philosophy by charting the ingredients of both.

Theologian: The first four ingredients on the chart must be included in any attempt at a definition of religion.

	RELIGION		PHILOSOPHY
1.	Beliefs, a credo, based on faith	1.	Teachings based on reason
2.	Worship according to a ritual	2.	No worship, no ritual
3.	A transformation of the individual to a higher degree of spirituality	3.	A transformation of the individual to a higher degree of understanding
4.	A group	4.	A group
5.	A Bible, the source of religion	5.	A book, the source of a philosophy
6.	Salvation, the goal	6.	Enlightenment, the goal
7.	Prayers, sacraments	7.	None
8.	A leader with authority	8.	A teacher or books

Timothy:	What's a religious sect? I realize that sect may not strictly relate to the chart.
Theologian:	A religious sect is a group of people who break away from a mainstream religion, like the Protestant religion, in order to live a stricter religious life, like the Amish.
Juan:	What is a religious cult?
Theologian:	A religious cult is a smaller group than a sect. Cultic members also break away from a mainstream religion. Their intention is to live one particular belief that is at odds with the belief system of the main religion. A charismatic leader dominates the group in its teachings and ritual worship. The satanic cult, which invokes the power of hate over enemies, is a notorious example of a cult. P. S. Since there are no accepted definitions these are only rough definitions of sect and cult.
Rosemary:	I don't think it's as important to remember the difference between a sect and a cult as it is to remember the difference between religion and philosophy.
Ivan:	I'll remember the difference this way. If I were to ask, "Does the devil exist?" the theologian will reply, "My Bible says yes." The philosopher will reply, "My reason says no."
Violetta:	Before prima donna Philosophy struts off the stage, she ought to

define herself. What is philosophy? My appetite is not satisfied with that chart of ingredients.

Philosopher: Since philosophers define themselves differently, let's adopt one of their definitions. Philosophy is a discipline that asks the widest possible questions the human mind is capable of thinking. For example, what is the broadest idea, the umbrella idea, under which all other ideas are considered? The answer is "being," a thing that exists either in physical reality like a tree or in the mind like a thought. Everything, be it physical or mental, is a kind of "being," something that exists.

Violetta: I'm sorry I asked. Now I can appreciate why you say in the preface that you will omit the impractical problems of philosophy.

Philosopher: The nerve center of a philosopher's heart, Violetta is this. Philosophers have traditionally preened themselves as objective thinkers. Aristotle preached that just as the stomach is designed to digest food and not stones, so is the intellect shaped to digest evidence and not feelings. The all-star Greek meant that if a person is presented evidence his intellect must accept it regardless of any contrary, life-long opinion, feeling or prejudice. That's not easy to swallow. No one is 100% objective. We are all prejudiced to some degree. The more objective a person is the more philosophical he is.

Miss Ethics

Miss Ethics: I'm Miss Ethics or you can call me Miss Morals.

Sam: I frequently see morals and ethics together like twins. Are they different?

Philosopher: They are often used interchangeably. Morals deal with right and wrong conduct, e.g., would it be immoral for Carla to cheat in exams if her parents assigned so many household chores that she didn't have time to study? Ethics deal with the abstract rule and theories about right and wrong. For instance, should my ethical rule be the greatest good for the greatest number? (See chap.21.)

Caroline: I can remember the difference better between morals and ethics if you give me a "people" answer.

Philosopher: At your service. Some moralists were Jesus, Mahatma Gandhi, Martin Luther King, Jr. Some ethicians are the college philosophers who teach ethics.

Juan: How does religion differ from morals? Are they twins or cousins?

Miss Morals: To visualize the difference between religion and morals, picture Billy, who attends church on Sunday, recites his prayers, reads the Bible, believes in the truths of his faith. That's religion. Now picture the same Billy who during the week obeys his parents, treats his siblings kindly in word and deed, helps his neighbor to mow the lawn,

Theologian: volunteers one afternoon a week to work on a project for the homeless. That's morals.

Theologian: Another scenario to differentiate religion from morals is to visualize Mr. Sting acting religiously on Sunday in church but acting immorally during the rest of the week by lying, stealing, and bullying his neighbors. I might footnote that the Ten Commandments mold the moral backbone of the Jewish religion. The Christian religion accepts the same Ten Commandments plus other teachings especially Jesus' sermon on the mount.

Clarence: Is there any difference between morals in religion and morals in philosophy? If, for example, I were to ask a theologian and a philosopher this moral question, "Is it immoral to steal a neighbor's bicycle?" Wouldn't both agree that stealing is wrong?

Theologian: Yes, but their source for saying stealing is wrong would differ. The theologian would quote his Bible. The philosopher would consult his reason as his source and reply something like his — to steal the neighbor's bicycle would be contrary to justice and a violation of his right to private property. Of course, the theologian would agree.

Working Out

1. Is attendance at church, synagogue, temple or mosque a religious or moral act? Explain.

2. When you stop your car at a red light, are you making a) a moral stop, b) an ethical stop, c) a philosophical stop, d) a theological stop, e) all of the above, f) none of the above. Choose one answer and explain it.

3. If you were to tap a philosopher on the shoulder and inquire, "Do angels exist?" What "source" would he use to answer? How do you think he would answer — yes or no? If you posed the same question to a theologian what "source" would he use to answer? How do you think he would answer — yes or no?

4. A conversation between an astronaut and a believer:

   Astronaut: I flew higher than any earthling and I never saw God. What's more I have 20-20 vision.

   Believer: There is nothing wrong with your eyes but with your head. You will never see God no matter how high you fly. The evidence for his existence cannot be acquired through the senses. The biblical God is all spirit, not matter. A human being can only know God through his faith in the Bible. Have a nice day! (See chap. 11 on God's existence.)

5. Compose a conversation illustrating the same type of misunderstanding. For instance, a person tries to prove a biblical belief (the existence of heaven) through the senses.

Miss Bible

"The Bible was translated so many times that nobody knows what it means." That's a common uneducated remark to dismiss the Bible from a discussion. On the contrary a Bible (Hebrew, Christian, Muslim, etc.) may be legitimately introduced into a discussion after an agreement that the Bible wears three "veils:" the original text, translations, and interpretations.

THE ORIGINAL TEXT

Let's pick up the Christian Bible as an example of the three veils. This Bible houses a miniature library divided into the Old Testament and the New Testament.

The "original text" refers to the very first manuscript(s) written by the first author(s). Every original manuscript of every book in the Bible has perished.

Before the original texts wore out, scribes had copied them. Later scribes copied the manuscripts of previous scribes and so on down the centuries. The scribes first wrote on fragile papyri and later on parchments. Relief came in the 1400s, the dawn of the invention of printing in the Western world.

Textual scholars feverishly hunted down the oldest Old Testament Hebrew-Aramaic manuscripts and New Testament Greek manuscripts all over Europe and the Middle East. Then they busied themselves in the reconstruction of the original text of each biblical book as accurately as possible.

TRANSLATIONS

The second veil of the Bible is its translations. Scholars like Sherlock Holmes with magnifying glass in hand searched for the oldest biblical translations made from Hebrew-Aramaic and Greek into ancient languages, e.g., Syriac. Their happy hunting grounds were the medieval monasteries of Europe.

Of what value are translations? Scholars read them in order to detect what the Hebrew-Aramaic, Greek words most likely were. For example, if you found a translation into English from a French manuscript and your eyes fell upon the words, "I have hunger" instead of "I am hungry" you would instantly conclude that the original lost French manuscript read "J'ai faim."

After the roundup of all the oldest Hebrew-Aramaic, Greek manuscripts and old translations of the Bible into various ancient languages, scholars struggle to restore the original texts word for word. The result is the critical text of the Bible.

From this critical text all translations are made into modern languages: English, Italian, Spanish, French, German, Chinese, etc. Professional translators must know well both the biblical language from which they translate and the modern language into which they translate. The same professional translators do not allow religious beliefs to influence their translations. Such an influence would be considered below their scholarly dignity. To select the most precise modern language word to translate a Hebrew-Aramaic, Greek word is an objective, honorable duty. Regardless of how objectively translators toil, they are forever humbly remindful of the Italian proverb, "a translator is a traitor." ("traduttore, traditore")

INTERPRETATIONS

Interpretation begins only after the Bible is translated. An interpretation is the meaning given by the reader to the translated words. At the Last Supper, for instance, Jesus said, "This is my body, this is my blood." The statement is the translation from the Greek, but what does it mean? What's its interpretation? Commentators dispute: did Jesus mean "body" and "blood" in the physical sense or in the symbolic sense? The battle of interpretation is now engaged. (There is hardly a statement that falls from our lips, which cannot be interpreted differently.)

SUMMARY

There exists near-perfect agreement among scholars on the original text and on most professional translations but definitely not on interpretations. Biblical scholars do not interpret meanings from a translation but from the critical Hebrew-Aramaic, Greek Bible. Non-scholars wisely use a translated Bible with footnotes wherever there is a dispute about the translation of Hebrew-Aramaic, Greek words.

A Diagram Summary of the Three Biblical Veils

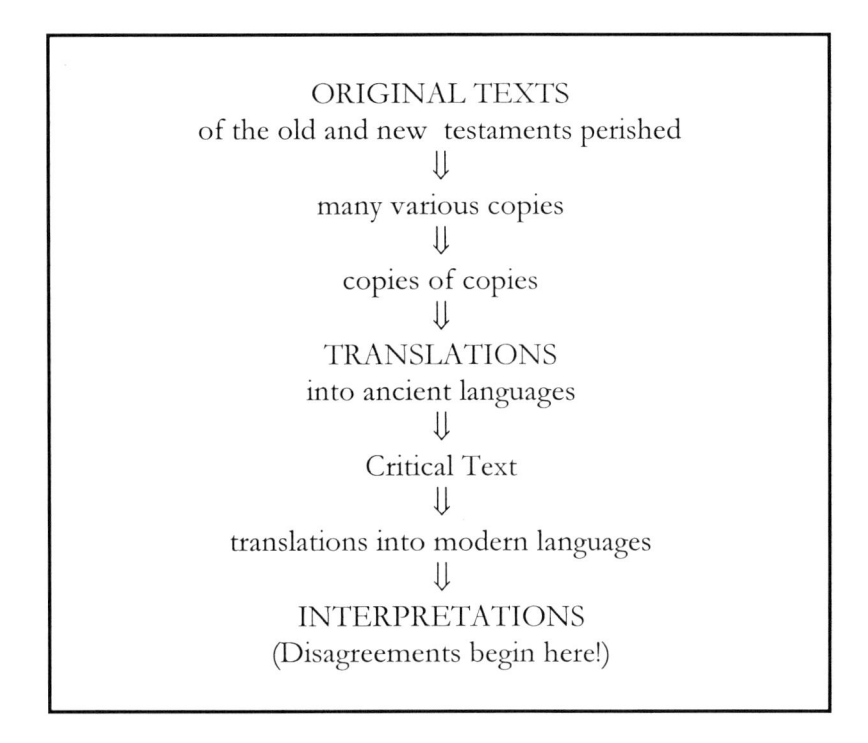

ORIGINAL TEXTS
of the old and new testaments perished
⇓
many various copies
⇓
copies of copies
⇓
TRANSLATIONS
into ancient languages
⇓
Critical Text
⇓
translations into modern languages
⇓
INTERPRETATIONS
(Disagreements begin here!)

Biblical Gymnastics

1. Are there any original texts still existing? Circle yes or no.

2. Define original text.

3. Why are translations from the three original languages into other ancient languages important for scholars to restore the original texts?

4. Prior to interpreting a biblical passage, what two "veils" should command your agreement? Explain.

5. What does the critical text mean or why is it important?

6. What makes a translator a professional?

7. Write a two-page essay of your thoughts about the following statement: the Bible was translated so many times that nobody knows what it means.

How to Interpret the Bible

"You can prove anything from the Bible." Purveyors of this negative statement have never heard of the science of hermeneutics, the rules of interpretation of written documents. These rules apply equally to a letter from a sweetheart, to a novel, poem, play, even to the Constitution of the United States. These rules are also used by all biblical scholars, whether they are fundamentalists or critical scholars. Even English literature graduate students are familiar with hermeneutics.

First rule, what is the literary form of the particular biblical book in question? It is of primary importance to establish the literary form because each literary form has its own truth. Each literary form expresses its meaning differently. The biblical books are written in a variety of literary forms. The Books of Kings are written in the literary form of history, the Psalms in poetry, the Book of Ruth and the four Gospels in the form of biographies, the books of the major and minor prophets in the form of oratorical literature. The writings of St. Paul are in the epistolary form.

Second rule, the scholar has to find out the meaning of the original Old Testament Hebrew-Aramaic, and New Testament Greek words.

Third rule, is the translation as accurate as possible?

Fourth rule, what do the original Hebrew-Aramaic, Greek words mean in their context in the sentence? This rule is violated when the words are taken out of context and made to mean something which the writers never intended.

Fifth rule, if the words are unclear in the immediate context, the reader searches in the previous and following sentences to understand the meaning of the words. If unclear, the reader looks for the meaning of the word in other writings of the same author and in writings of contemporary authors. Bear in mind that there were no Hebrew-Aramaic, Greek dictionaries until after the entire Bible was written, (ca. A.D. 125).

Sixth rule, the scholar seeks to learn how the Hebrew-Aramaic, Greek words were translated in other languages.

Seventh rule, the scholar asks, "When was the book written? For what type of audience? Why was it written?"

Eight rule, what were the historical and cultural backgrounds of the writer?

We may stop at this juncture of the incomplete list of hermeneutical rules and inquire, "If there is so much agreement on the above rules between Christian fundamentalists and Christian critical biblical scholars, why do they differ in their interpretations of so many passages in the Bible?" The simple answer is that they differ in their interpretations because they differ in their understanding of biblical inerrancy, the belief that the Bible cannot err. Both groups believe in biblical inspiration, that God inspired the biblical writers. The critical scholars claim that there cannot be any error in matters of religion; the fundamentalists believe that there cannot be any error whatsoever in the entire Bible including all the secular disciplines of science, math, history, geography, etc. (To continue the dispute would lead us into the thickets of theology and beyond the confines of this book.)

LOGIC

CHAPTER 4

Are Science And Religion Still Boxing? The Scopes Trial

"Science is organized knowledge."

Herbert Spencer

An Imaginary Dialogue between Galileo and a Fundamentalist

Chairperson: You heard scientists broadcasting that their most fruitful instrument to fish for knowledge is the senses (chap.1). You listened to philosophers who bellowed that their best instrument to hunt for knowledge is reason (chaps. 2 & 3). You bumped into the stocky theologians who informed you that their principal tool to dig for knowledge is the Bible. Therefore, you now logically ask why are scientists and theologians still boxing one another's ears if each team has its own special instrument to answer its own set of questions? Your logical implication is that they should hang up their gloves. To answer your question in high drama I invited Galileo to represent the scientists and a 21st century fundamentalist to represent the theologians.

Galileo: The most celebrated boxing match in history between a team of scientists vs. theologians dates back to my time in the 1600s. Two rough looking theologians, with a search warrant from the Vatican's Inquisition Department, ordered me to stand trial for teaching a doctrine contrary to the Bible. The Bible assumes that the earth is the center of the universe and the sun revolves around it. I performed various experiments to advance the view that, on the contrary, it's the earth that revolves around the sun. My knock out argument was the telescope, a recent invention that I had imported from the Netherlands.

Fundamentalist: Stop boasting and tell us who won the boxing match.

Galileo: The theologians of course. Not because they refuted my scientific arguments but because they wielded a big Papal stick.

Fundamentalist: A big Papal stick?

Galileo: Yes, they could have burned me at the stake. They could have locked me up in the Inquisition jail. Instead, they carried me back to my beloved city of Florence where I remained under house arrest for the rest of my life.

Fundamentalist: So you recanted and became a born-again Christian by accepting the literal meaning of the Bible?

Galileo: No. Never. I thought that the Catholics would grow up and accept the facts of science if I could explain them properly. I failed to convince the Vatican officials.

Fundamentalist: And so the Catholics continued to interpret the Bible literally, as we fundamentalists still do today?

Galileo: For the following centuries, up to the 1900s Catholics and Protestants continued to interpret the Bible literally. Meanwhile they hampered us scientists from performing experiments to improve the physical conditions and health of the human race. (1) Was there afterwards a trial as famous as mine?

Fundamentalist: Yes, the Scopes Trial of 1925. It also dealt with the literal interpretation of the Bible. However, this time the boxing match was about creation and evolution.

Galileo: So the ghost of the Scopes Trial is alive and well in its new dress of creationism. It's the same old story of you theologians sticking your fingers in the holes of the dike to prevent the tide of science. In the creationist controversy, you literal interpreters are trying to muscle your way into public schools to make converts and turn students away from the theory of evolution. We scientists interpret the world objectively without a preconceived idea. You interpret the world subjectively with a preconceived biblical idea.

Fundamentalist: That's an unchristian way of painting the scene.

Galileo: I heard through the heavenly grapevine — or the other one — that the liberal Protestants, the Roman Catholics and critical Jewish

	biblical scholars found the key to biblical interpretation over 50 years ago. It's uncomplicated. God inspired the biblical writers only in religious matters not in secular matters of science, history, geography, and so on. As to the creation of humans, the same three groups of critical biblical scholars interpret the Bible to mean that God created everything and everybody but as to HOW God created — through evolution or whatever — is a scientific question to be decided by scientists. I once heard those critical scholars sing an old tune. "The Bible teaches how to go to heaven not how the heavens go." If only I had known that tune I would have serenaded the Vatican officials with it.
Fundamentalist:	A lot of good that trite tune would have done you. We have a richer tune. "If it was good enough for Jonah, it's good enough for me." For your information the critical interpretation of the Bible that you just outlined is anathema to us literal interpreters just as it was to the Vatican inquisitors of your day. We kept the faith. We interpret the Bible just as it reads. If the Bible says God made man from the slime of the earth that's what it means. Once you begin changing what the Bible means there is no end to it till the meaning of the whole Bible is destroyed.
Galileo:	If I could not convince the Inquisition toughies, I'll never convince

you. By the way, it's sunset. My space rocket is arriving over the horizon. Before I return to my heavenly cell, let's answer the students' question like this. We scientists and you theologians should stick to our set of questions respectively and hang up our boxing gloves. One last thought. From my 1600s till today, you theologians began more fights than we did. Most of your fights were based on a literal interpretation of the Bible. Nevertheless, we scientists will continue to read and understand Mother Nature and her universe with our experiments not with a book written prior to the birth of modern science. Meanwhile for entertainment, we'll watch on the interplanetary Internet who will win the next boxing match between you literalists and your opponents the critical interpreters. Farewell.

Unknown philosopher's email: In my unsolicited opinion, scientists and theologians should adopt this motto. Render to Science the things that are Science and to God the things that are God's.

The Scopes Trial

"There is no error so monstrous that it fails to find defenders among the ablest men."

Lord Acton

A NEWS FLASHBACK

In March 1925 the State of Tennessee prohibited the teaching (in public schools) of all theories contrary to the biblical account of creation. John T. Scopes, a biology teacher in Dayton, Tennessee, was tried in July of that year for teaching evolution.

Clarence Darrow defended Scopes. William Jennings Bryan opposed. The trial electrified the nation. The two lawyers were national icons. Darrow argued that the Tennessee legislature took the side of religion and therefore was in violation of the separation of church and state. He criticized Bryan's literal interpretation of the Bible. Scopes was convicted but later released. The Scopes Trial cast its ghostly shadow down to our own days. The controversy has not drawn its last breath. End of news flashback.

Today

If Darrow and Bryan were debating today, they would upgrade their arguments and sound like this:

Darrow: I see that you have never given up attempts to teach the Genesis account of creation in public schools since our spectacular drawn-out debate in 1925.

Bryan: You see correctly.

Darrow: I also hear that your goal all along the 20th century has been to get equal time with the teaching of evolution in the public classroom.

Bryan: You hear correctly.

Darrow: I read in a newspaper that you now plume yourselves as creationists.

Bryan: You read correctly. We creationists have scored many scientific hits against the theory of evolution. We exposed the hoax of the so-called Peking Man. In addition we are right on target when we protest that high school science instructors often teach, or give the impression, that evolution is a fact instead of a theory.

Darrow: It's not the fault of scientists if high school teachers present evolution as a fact instead of a theory. Incidentally, you should stress to your followers that scientists admit that they have not yet located the major missing link between the highest evolved type of an animal and the lowest evolved type of a human being. If they did they would hold a parade and elevate evolution from the category of a theory to that of a fact. Until that banner day scientists claim that the available evidence can be best interpreted by the theory of evolution.

Bryan: As if I didn't know that already! That's not my main concern. It's hard to gain entrance by teaching creationism (intelligent design) not as a religious doctrine-that God created the first couple as Genesis relates — but as an alternate scientific teaching to evolution.

Darrow: Since 1925 all your rewordings, disguises, have failed to convince both state and federal governments. You remain defiant?

Byran: Yes. We shall overcome! Let's agree to meet again in three years.

Darrow: Agreed! (Both shake hands as they look the other way.)

Evolving Exercises

1. Explain the difference between the literal and the critical interpretation of the Bible as you understand it.

2. Some religions refuse the help of modern medicine because it conflicts with the literal interpretation of the Bible. The Jehovah Witnesses at times refuse blood transfusions because they claim that the Bible forbids them. Another religion, not known for its friendliness towards modern medicine is Mary Baker Eddy's Christian Science. Do you know of any other religion, which forbids the use of modern science because of the literal meaning of the Bible?

3. Explain two similarities between Galileo's trial and the Scopes Trial.

4. Explain two differences between Galileo's trial and the Scopes Trial.

5. Comment on the epigraph.

CHAPTER 5

I'm Too Young To Think Logically

"Logic and rhetoric (make men) able to contend."

Francis Bacon

Those Irritating Definitions

Isabella: Teacher, before you define logic please brief us on definitions and tell us why they irritate.

Marcia: I know why they irritate. Yesterday I was speeding along for ten minutes about my favorite classical novels when Myra stopped me with, "Define a classic." Was I irritated! I don't know anyone who does not get irritated when asked to define what they are talking about.

Teacher: Thank you Marcia. The first commandment of any logical conversation or discussion states, "You shall define your terms." There are three types of definitions. Here they are in their own words.

Sir Stan: I'm a standard dictionary definition. I report on how people use words. As a bonus I label meanings as obsolete, colloquial, and slang.

Sir Theo: I'm a theoretical definition. I support a theory. If, for example, you search for the word drama you will first find the standard definition and then you will find me saying, "to teach a social problem." That's a theoretical definition because there are other theories about what a drama is.

Sir Genus: I'm a genus-species definition. You won't find me in dictionaries. I follow Aristotle's style of defining as exemplified in his celebrated definition of man as a rational animal. Man belongs to the genus animal and rational belongs to the species or specific difference. Man is an animal (genus) who reasons (species). Botanists and zoologists classify their plants and animals according to genus and species. These scientists are models for clarity of definition.

Lee: The rest of us mortals are not expected to toss off definitions according to genus and species in the course of conversation. I see this rigid type of definition as a useful tool when you want to be 100% clear about something.

Alice: I agree with Lee but I want a couple more examples of genus-species to impress my father at dinner tonight.

Teacher: A psychotic is a mentally ill person — genus or larger class — who has lost contact with reality to a considerable degree — species or smaller class. Another example is whenever you use an adjective describing a noun, you are classifying by genus and species. Verdi composed the immortal — adjective, species — opera — noun, genus Aida to celebrate the opening of the Suez Canal.

How to Sharpen Definitions

"My definition (of a philosopher) is of a man up in a balloon, with his family and friends holding the ropes which confine him to earth and trying to haul him down."

Louisa May Alcott

1. A useful definition expresses the essential not the accidental. A musician is a person who plays an instrument (essential). A musician is a person who has a beard and long hair (accidental).

2. It is repetitious to use the same term in a definition as the word to be defined. A beautiful girl is one who is adorned with beauty.

3. To define with a synonym is not informative. A car is an automobile.

4. Figurative definitions are more appreciated in literature than in logic, which prefers literal, straight language.

    Teacher: Define a socialist government.

    Tatiana: A government that hasn't got its act together.

    Teacher: A first class figurative definition and an excuse for not thinking.

5. The task of a definition is to clarify what a word means rather than what it

does not mean.

Teacher: For tomorrow's homework define a poem and don't tell me it's not a musical

Dottie: But aren't some words properly defined negatively?

Teacher: Yes. Name two.

Dottie: Widow and widower.

Teacher: Three cheers for Dottie!

6. Definitions that are too broad weaken their meaning. Athletes often throw around the word philosophy to signify "strategy" as in "We'll win tomorrow because we will adopt a new philosophy of tackling."

How to Recognize an Argument

"Truth is the cry of all, but the game of the few."

George Berkeley

Introduction

An intelligent argument or conversation not only requires a definition of terms and an awareness of fallacies but also demands a sound construction. If an argument was a house furnished with the gift of speech, it would describe its construction like this, "My house, argument, contains three floors. The first floor is called assumption (s), the second, premise(s), the third, conclusion. Come up and visit me sometime."

A Visit to the House of Argument

First floor: An assumption is "the act of…supposing that a thing is true…something that is taken for granted: supposition," (Webster's dictionary). Every argument sets out with one or more unspoken assumptions. Let's listen to an argument heating up at a bus stop.

Mr. Bruno: Italian is the most musical language in the world.

Mr. Toshiba: Sorry to contradict, Signore, but Japanese is the most musical language in the world.

From the very beginning of this argument an assumption made by both men is that they agree on what a language is: they are discussing a particular kind of language, a musical one.

A caveat: Sometimes you may not agree with the assumption (s) made by the other party. You must say so. In addition, note well that it's of philosophical importance to realize that the ultimate assumption made in any and every argument is the principle of contradiction: something cannot both be true and false at the same time and from the same point of view.

Second floor: A premise is a statement often recognizable by telltale words: because, since, given that, for, inasmuch as, for as much as, owing to, on account of, whereas.

Third floor: A conclusion is a statement often recognizable by telltale words: therefore, wherefore, consequently, so, accordingly, as a result, hence, ergo. Either the premise or the conclusion may begin a sentence containing an argument. The most puzzling section of the house of argument is to find the stairway between the second and third floors: does the conclusion truly flow from the premise(s)?

Exercise on Assumptions

Indicate one assumption in each of the three following statements:

1. I don't recall the last time you drove under the influence.
2. I don't have the amount of money that you would accept to spy on your country.
3. You told me yesterday how long you were going to give up drinking this time.

Exercise on Arguments

In the following arguments identify the premise by underlining it with one line and identify the conclusion by underlining it with two lines. (Sample: <u>Because he scored A's in math,</u> <u><u>I therefore thought that he would choose computer studies as his major.</u></u>

Since Liz spells so well, we accordingly bet our last silver dollar that she would win the national spelling contest.

Given that I'm from Detroit, the car capital of the world, I can consequently repair your Ford.

Theodore Roosevelt advocated the expulsion of conscientious objectors from our country for no man who won't pull his weight in the boat has no right in the boat.

Debate

Should drugs be legalized? Yes vs. No. Indicate assumptions, premises, conclusions.

An Expression Trip

Here are four commonly used expressions during discussions:

Possible vs. Probable	"It's possible" is a minimal concession. It simply means that there is no strict contradiction in a statement or idea. "It's probable" is a sizeable concession. It means that there are enough reasons or evidence to establish an opinion. The probability (or opinion) may range from most probable to least probable.
In Principle	The frequently used expression "they agree in principle" signifies that they agree about the basics but not the details. The latter are discussed later.
Prima Facie	These two Latin words, meaning "at first view" have the same meaning when used in English. Some synonyms are "apparently" or "at first impression." A prima facie duty, for example, is an apparent or self-evident duty. Lawyers

	use the expression "prima facie evidence" to specify that the evidence is so apparent that it needs no further proof.
A Value Judgment	A fact is objective. A value judgment is subjective. If a reliable scale indicates that a cat weighs ten pounds, the proud owner may state it as a fact. When Magdalena declares, "My cat is beautiful, friendly, companionable," she is announcing value judgments.

Exercises

1. Write four sentences exemplifying your mastery of the four expressions above.

2. Why would this axiom make sense to you? He who asserts must prove.

"I wish he would explain his explanation."

Lord Byron

An intelligent conversation/discussion/debate sparkles if it's dressed up with a clear definition of terms, an awareness of a well-structured argument (with premises and conclusion), an alertness of the difference between an argument and an explanation.

An argument aims to prove or disprove. An explanation aims to describe or narrate. Following is Tom's example of an explanation. "Last summer I toured the historical city of Verona, Italy. One of its famous attractions, besides the tomb of Romeo and Juliet, is the ancient Roman arena where summer operas are staged. After the performance of Verdi's opera, A Masked Ball, when the arena was almost empty, I copied from the walls some of the Latin graffiti dating back to Roman times. I intended to show them to my Latin teacher in Chicago."

Tom's tour is not an argument because there is no premise and conclusion to prove or disprove anything. There is only a narrative or description of his visit.

Explanatory Exercises

Give one reason why the following are not arguments but explanations:

1. Leonardo da Vinci's Mona Lisa (in the Louvre Museum in Paris) is the most famous talked about painting in the history of art. There are barrels of theories trying to explain her smile.

2. Last Saturday night as Herb stood on the threshold of the dance floor, his business mind took in the following inventory: Donald's girlfriend was elegant; Edgar's girlfriend was over-dressed; Merlin's girlfriend was attractive; Harold's girlfriend was beautiful.

Homework

Write a one-page essay on your hobby. Include one explanation and two arguments.

CHAPTER 6

Superstitions but Fallacies? Superstitions? Me?

"The human reason is better adapted for the detection of errors than the discovery of positive truth."

Peter Bayle (1)

Are We Overdosing on Fallacies?

Roy: Before we define a fallacy, how does logic differ from thinking? Are thinkers and logicians roommates?

Logician: Thinking is an umbrella term covering a variety of mental activities — reasoning, imagining, remembering, believing, doubting, guessing, even daydreaming. Logic is concerned with only one form of thinking, which is called reasoning. Logic is a study of rules and methods of correct reasoning. Reasoning is a mental process of drawing a conclusion from premise(s). A fallacy is an error in reasoning or in drawing a conclusion from premise(s).

Warning: Not all fallacies are easy to detect. They often appear clothed in glittering truth. That's why they seduce reasoning. Facts: there is no agreement on the number of fallacies, their definitions, their names.

Fallacy of Small Sample

Simon: My dear Constance, you are the most beautiful girl in the world.

Constance: You just committed the fallacy of small sample. Have you seen all the girls in the world? Don't you remember the two important rules for correct sampling?

Simon: No.

Constance: The sampling must be large. How large? As large as it takes. And varied. How varied? As varied as it takes. Therefore before making your statement you should have seen a large sample of girls and girls of many varieties.

Fallacy of Generalization

The generalization fallacy surfaces when a person says "everyone" or "everything" and fails to realize that only one exception makes the statement wrong.

Mr. Wong: Have you noticed that all of us Chinese have small noses and all Americans have big noses?

Daughter: Daddy, all I have to do is find one Chinese with a big nose and one American with a small nose to prove you wrong.

Mr. Wong: Happy hunting!

Fallacy of Ad Hominem (Latin "to the man")

Ad Hominem is the fallacy of attacking an opponent personally instead of refuting his statements.

Native American: The U. S. Government broke land treaties made with my ancestors.

White Supremacist: Your ancestors never knew how to cultivate land anyway.

Fallacy of Ad Baculum (Latin "to the stick")

Ad Baculum is the fallacy of threatening physical force instead of offering a pertinent reply. For example, when the American colonists refused taxation without representation the English authorities replied with an argument Ad Baculum by dispatching English redcoats to quell the rebellion.

Fallacy of Appeal to False Authority

This label refers to the fallacy of attributing competency to a person who lacks it though competent in something else.

Olympic swimmer on TV: How did I win my gold medal? I ate Wheaties for breakfast.

Laura to mother: May we switch to Wheaties for breakfast?

Teacher: How did Laura fall into the fallacy of appeal to false authority?

Justin: Laura believed the swimmer who attributed the cause of her gold medal to Wheaties.

Teacher: Correct! Laura appealed to the swimmer, an authority on swimming, as if she were also an authority on Wheaties.

Fallacy of Post Hoc (Latin "after this")

A person is lured into the fallacy of post hoc by asserting that a second event was caused by a first event, when the second event merely followed the first chronologically. For example, suppose a Spanish newspaper screamed these headlines: "Forest fires spread after North African refugees swam to our shores." The implication is that the fires (the second event) were caused by the refugees who swam on shore (the first event). In reality, other probabilities were lightning storms or Spanish picnickers who caused the fires.

Fallacy of Inconsistency

Teacher: Would you respect a person who voiced one opinion yesterday and a contradictory opinion today?

Herman: It all depends on whether he got new evidence today that he did not have yesterday.

Teacher: Brilliant answer, Herman! Here is another example. If a congressman declared yesterday on the floor of the House of Representatives that he favored the "Star War" project and informed the press today that he was against it without offering new evidence, he would be committing the fallacy of inconsistency.

Fallacy of Suppressed Evidence

Most fallacies are buried in the basket labeled "suppressed evidence." All fallacies suppress some amount of evidence. Yet, one such fallacy is so popular on TV and radio that it merits a special airing. We may nickname it "the no-better fallacy."

How often have our ears been buffeted by a victorious commercial voice crooning at the finale of a sales pitch "no product is better" or "nothing is better."

First a peek-a-boo background. It's the cherished dream of every company in the competitive jungle to announce to the city and to the world that its product is "the best," heads and shoulders above its rivals. There is only one roadblock. Most companies don't produce "the best." If they did they would publicize it noisily from the store tops. Consequently a company cautiously words its ad to mean it's "the best" without literally saying so. This legal deceit sidesteps a lie, a suit, and government penalties.

Shoppers will conclude that the expression means this product is the best even though the literal meaning says that no product is better because others are just as good. The suppressed evidence is hiding in the last six unspoken words.

Fallacy of Two Wrongs Make A Right

This designation refers to the fallacy of justifying a wrong action because others do it.

Principal:	Tim, you know the rule applies equally to all. If you're late for class, you are to remain after school for one hour. Why are you tardy?
Tim:	Other students are late.
Teacher:	Tim was washed away by this fallacy because he drew a wrong conclusion. He thought that he was justified in his tardiness — the conclusion — because others were late — the premise. The others were wrong and Tim was also wrong. Two wrongs don't make a right.

Fallacy of Appeal to Consensus

The appeal to consensus fallacy occurs when people proclaim that everyone they know agrees about something.

Sara: Of course astrology is true!

Jane: Wait! Let's define astrology according to Webster's dictionary. "Astrology — a divination that treats of the supposed influences of the stars upon human affairs and of foretelling terrestrial events by their positions and aspects."

Sara: As I was saying, all my friends say astrology is true and so do the newspapers, magazines, and talk shows.

Jane: You just flopped into the fallacy of appeal to consensus. Instead of attempting to prove that stars influence human affairs you simply appealed to a consensus.

Unknown philosopher: I reject astrology for this reason. How come that people born under the same star at the same time and in the same place are different? (Silence dominates.)

Omar: The polls are the most popular fallacy of appeal to consensus.

Teacher: Excellent! Yes, just because the polls indicate that 60% are for and 40% against a proposition does not signify that the 60% are more correct than the 40%. The polls do not reflect the reasons why people choose for or against a proposition. Many people vote out of feeling rather than reason. Therefore to say that 60% are correct is to say, "I appeal to consensus as a standard of truth."

Fallacy of non sequitur (Latin "It does not follow")

A non sequitur fallacy jumps up when a person concludes illogically from a premise(s). "It" the conclusion, does not follow. (Strictly speaking, a non sequitur applies to all fallacies but some fallacies are so clearly "non-follows" that they deserve the lion's share of the title.)

A notorious non sequitur is that of Erich von Daniken's <u>Chariots of the Gods.</u> He claims that because there is no scientific explanation for several phenomena (e.g., the giant stone statues on Easter Island, the airfield in the Andes mountains) therefore they are explainable by extraterrestrial visitors. The conclusion is a non sequitur. His conclusion should logically have been "We don't know the answer." To have concluded logically, von Daniken should have offered some evidence for the visit of extraterrestrials.

Fallacious Exercises

1. Give one example of each of the ten fallacies explained above.
2. Write a fallacy couched in a TV ad you recently heard.
3. Do you agree or disagree with the rejection of astrology as expressed by the unknown philosopher? (See above under the fallacy of appeal to consensus.)
4. Find one example of the ten fallacies above in your favorite newspapers/magazines.
5. Write a conversation about a boy in love with a girl. Place four fallacies in

the mouth of the boy without mentioning the name of the fallacies. Instruct the girl to identify the fallacies and explain to him why they are fallacies.

6. The girl is to reverse the process outlined in number five above.

Superstitions? Me?

Rookie logicians will consider superstitions "infra dignitatem" (Latin "beneath their dignity"). Why this snobbery? Simple. After a study of fallacies rookie logicians will be on the lookout for violations of the law of causality, the law of cause and effect. If they stumble upon a superstition they will be more prone to ask, "Is that an actual cause of that effect? Where is the proof?" Take the first superstition listed below. Redheads have hot tempers. Does the fact that a person who has red hair (the alleged cause) cause that person to have a hot temper (the effect)? Where is the proof? Is this a popular belief? Am I, a junior logician, expected to accept it? Is it not "infra dig?"

Exercises

Apply the law of cause and effect (there is no effect without a cause) to the 20 superstitions below. See if you can explain that in each of the 20 superstitions the law of cause and effect has been violated. Or, you may prefer to explain the superstitions with the help of one of Webster's definitions of superstition, namely, "a belief, conception, act, or practice resulting from ignorance, unreasoning, fear of an unknown or mysterious, morbid scrupulosity, trust in magic or chance or a false conception of causation, a fixed irrational idea, a notion maintained in spite of evidence to the contrary." An easier option is to explain each superstition as a false conclusion drawn from a premise.

1. Redheads have a hot temper.

2. Good or bad things come in threes. (Refutation: If you keep counting good or bad things, they will come in fours, fives, etc.)

3. You will enjoy good luck if your first or last name contains seven letters.

4. Thirteen is an unlucky number. For example, don't accept a hotel room on the 13th floor.

5. If you accidentally drop a fork on the floor, a female will soon visit. If you drop a knife, a male will visit.

6. You attract bad luck if you walk or run under a ladder.

7. If you spill some salt accidentally, throw a dash of it over your left shoulder to prevent bad luck.

8. You can prevent an evil if you cross your fingers.

9. If you trip over a threshold upon entering a house, reenter to prevent bad luck.

10. If a stray bird flies into a house, one of its inhabitants will die within a year.

11. If you chance upon a wishbone, you and your dining companion may make a wish. Each one pulls on the wishbone, the wish will come true for the person who broke off the larger piece.

12. Make a child eat garlic and voila! No more bed-wetting.

13. Hang a necklace of garlic on the wall and good luck will walk into your house.

14. Rub your hand over a bald-headed man to help you remember answers for examination questions.

15. A four-leaf clover brings luck.

16. You will be a lucky person if you are the seventh offspring (male or female) of the seventh offspring (male or female).

17. If you move from one house to another and take the broom with you, you will meet with bad luck.

18. If a crow caws near your home, beware because an evil is about to strike especially if you live in the country.

19. To sleep on the left side may eventually give you a heart attack. (Refutation: the heart is on the right side. It's internally well protected.)

20. If a woman is born with a V-shaped hairline, her husband will die while she is still young.

INTERLUDE

CHAPTER 7

The Media: Are Journalists Ethical? Trust Them? How Much?

"A newspaper that is true to its purpose concerns itself not only with the way things are but with the way they ought to be."

Joseph Pulitzer

An Ethician Interviews A Journalist

Ethician: What prelude have you to play on your fiddle before I drill you with embarrassing questions?

Journalist: We media personnel take our profession seriously. We influence the thinking, beliefs, values of the public both educated and uneducated. We influence their views be they political, religious, educational, economical, social or cultural.

Ethician: How do you paint yourself within the picture frame of democracy?

Journalist: As a supplier of information to citizens so that they can understand and participate in the democratic process; we inform them about whom to elect, what laws and policies to vote for. We deliver news about all affairs of the city, nation, and the world.

Ethician: How objectively may you write or speak when you realize that your employers depend on advertisers? Excuse the comparison, but don't you feel sometimes like hired guns?

Journalist:	We try to write and speak as independents, not as puppets manipulated by employers, the government, politicians, and advertisers.
Ethician:	How can you justify invading the privacy of celebrities?
Journalist:	Let's suppose that the invasion instructs the public how not to live immorally, how not to imitate the sexual activities and drug habits of famous people. Would we not be justified? (1)
Ethician:	Definitely not. The end does not justify the means in this case. Besides, who would give you this mandate as big brother? Certainly not the constitution nor the government.
Journalist:	The people have a right to know.
Ethician:	That's a much-abused slogan fabricated by you journalists when challenged. The people have a right to know about legitimate investigations. The slogan must not be shouted to justify any and every investigation that you consider sensational like prying on celebrities. How do photojournalists justify an explicit bias when they take a picture of a candidate in a ludicrous posture?
Journalist:	Maybe some photojournalists don't differentiate between bias and humor.
Ethician:	What would you say if the public demanded some degree of censorship of sex and violence in the news?

Journalist:	I would fight it.
Ethician:	Why not admit that your display of sex and violence is pandering to the lower appetites of the multitude in order to attract more viewers and readers for your advertisers?
Journalist:	We give the public what they want.
Ethician:	As journalists you are supposed to be elevating society not sinking to its lowest denominator for the sake of greenbacks. Let's move on. Are you aware of how flippantly some of you media people stereotype ethnic groups especially the poor ones without any clout?
Journalist:	Some colleagues might answer by pointing to the shortage of time on TV and radio and shortage of space in newspapers and magazines. (2)
Ethician:	Sorry. Those are frivolous excuses and unjustifiable.

How Much Can We Trust Them?

Why sound the alarm? Here's why. The information age is drowning us in an ocean of news. We desperately grasp for a lifeboat heading towards the shore of truth. We're drifting in a fog of uncertainty about which national or international corporation owns all the news media. We can see through the mist that those who control information control our minds. They sway our views about our institutions of government, politics, the economy, education, the military; they mold our tastes in food, drink, clothes, music, and entertainment. The dismal result is that informational control weakens us as democratic people. Control shapes us into puppets instead of critical thinkers required by a democracy.

As puppets we are bombarded with simple repetitions delivered in rapid images when we should be served with more news analyses. An unthinking public is the ultimate prize of controllers beaming skewed news from their towers of self-interest. In precooked news lies the poison pill of democracy.

Useful Hints for Consumers of News (3)

1. Switch on the news with the attitude of forming your own critical, not cynical opinion.

2. Never forge all your opinions on the anvil of only one source, be it one newspaper, one magazine, one TV channel, least of all one newscaster.

3. Since editorials are the most serious part of a newspaper, read them for their attempted analyses of local, national, international events, and personalities. Sometimes they are masterpieces.

4. Follow up the editorials with a reading of op-ed pieces by nationally known writers. You will notice that the editorials and op-ed writers are often either biased democrats or biased republicans. Gradually you will be able to predict their views on controversial topics without reading them.

5. Very few editors and syndicated columnists are scholars in their appointed specialties. At best they offer journalese scholarship, which differs from academic scholarship. Journalists are unsurpassable in the latest facts, eyewitness reports, up-to-date quotations from prominent world figures. Their Achilles' heel is their lack of background in which academic scholars abound. (4) In writing style journalists tower over academics. The latter are

superior in rigorous logic at the cost of dullness. Journalists would be surprised if they peeked into classrooms throughout the nation to hear professors reading media pieces to students for the sport of finding fallacies and unabashed biases.

6. Glance at the credits of the writers of the letters to the editor. Some are authorities. They may prove more knowledgeable and insightful than the editors or opinion writers in their suggestions, objections, refutations.

7. Ask yourself frequently whose interests are being served in this news piece? This attitude prevents a passive acceptance of the news as if it were the gospel truth.

8. Some of the best newspapers in the United States are reputed to be: The New York Times, The Washington Post, The Boston Globe, The Los Angeles Times, and The Christian Science Monitor in its news coverage which excludes its religious orientation.

9. The World Press magazine prints articles from the most respected newspapers and periodicals on the planet. What these articles frankly state about Americans and their policies either make us burst with pride or blush with shame.

10. If you are aware about which countries are closely tied to U. S. A. (England? Israel?) interpret American reports about those countries with a grain of salt, large size.

11. If you are aware about which countries are far from tied to U. S. A. due to the policies of whatever administration happens to be holding the reins of government, consume a grain of salt, extra large size.

12. If you know which unfriendly foreign countries pay lobbyists in our country to influence government officials in Washington, be on the lookout for favors requested and received by the foreign countries.

13. An ideal method of gathering information about what is truly going on in our own country might be the following: acquaint yourself with the ideology (the characteristic ideas) of the conservative Republicans, the liberal Democrats, and less importantly, the Independents, the Libertarians, the Natural Law Party.

Discussion

1. Can you think of any personal convictions you got from TV? Radio? Newspapers? Magazines? Would you care to share them?

2. What do you think the role of a journalist should be?

3. Are you satisfied/dissatisfied with the news media? Explain.

4. If the president appointed you the News Czar, how would you improve the news media?

5. Do you think that journalists have the right to invade the privacy of celebrities' lives as in the case of Diana Princess of Wales, August 1997?

6. Would you or would you not limit the defensive battle cry of the journalists, "The people have the right to know." Explain.

7. When an international or national controversy hits the headlines and the majority opinion is repeated daily do you find yourself automatically

accepting the majority view without any personal thinking?

8. Give two examples of how photojournalists can show bias in photos.

9. In your opinion should news coverage foresee problems and not only report problems? Give two examples.

10. Should there be some type of censorship on sex and violence in magazines, newspapers, TV in spite of the right of free speech? Explain.

11. Can you think of some unethical practices of the journalists not mentioned by the ethician in the interview above?

12. Advertisers should be prohibited from telling people what medications to take for ailments. That's the job of the doctor. Discuss.

13. Would you like to see more good news? Why? Give one example.

14. Give examples where you believe that the ethician was unfair to the journalist in the above interview.

15. In spite of the defects of the American news media, could you defend the view that it is the world's best? Second best? Just as good as any other nation's news media?

16. Comment on the epigraph.

CHAPTER 8

Who Am I?   Something? (Matter) Or Somebody? (Matter-Spirit)

"What a chimera then is man . . . the glory and shame of the universe."

Pascal

I fancy that every teenager at least once gazes into the mirror and vigorously brushing teeth whispers, "Who am I?"

The question is privately serious. It pops out of the hidden caves of the head and into the voice after the teenager has done something displeasing. It's a personal question, which the voice mixes into a bowl with other musings: "What do people expect from me? What do I expect from myself? Can I perform as expected?" It's tragic that some teenagers answer these questions with suicide.

I nurse the suspicion that if teenagers examine the philosophical question "Who am I?" they will find the personal question easier to face.

Thought:	Go email Rebecca an apology.
Question:	Where did that thought come from? Where do all my thoughts and feelings come from?
Brain:	From me (matter).
Brain:	From us (matter plus spirit).
Referee:	Everyone agrees that thoughts and feelings originate in the brain but

69

the controversy is this: do thoughts and feelings come only from the brain — which is matter, something physical — or do they also come from a non-material, non-physical reality called the spirit, soul, mind?

Materialist: We claim that all mental activity, all thoughts and feelings, come only from the brain. We accept the teachings of neurosurgeons, namely, that the brain houses a complex web of electric-chemical charges from which all our thoughts and feelings begin. In our view, when you command your body to walk to the computer to email a message, at that very moment physical movements occur in your brain. Moreover, neurosurgeons can even show you a physical movement taking place in your brain when you simply change opinion without uttering a word or moving a finger.

Believer: We believe that in addition to a physical, material brain, humans also possess a reality that is not physical, non-material, called a spirit or soul or mind that works together with the brain to produce thoughts and feelings. Furthermore, we assert that no neurosurgeon, regardless of his state-of-the-art searchlight, cannot actually see in the brain a thought speeding from one never center to another.

Materialist: That's correct, but neither can John Doe see radio waves whizzing in the air around him but they are there.

Referee: In both examples of the brain with its electric-chemical components and the example of the radio waves, there exists a type of energy, which is one variety of matter.

Student: So who won the debate, the materialist or the believer?

Referee: Neither won.

Exercises

1. Who do you think won the debate? Why?

2. Do you think that the philosophical question (is a human either all matter or matter plus spirit?) helps to answer the personal question, "Who am I?" Explain Yes or No.

3. Optional question: Did you ever ask yourself the personal question (Who am I?) as you brushed your teeth and looked in the mirror?

A Vignette

Am I influenced more by heredity or by environment?

This gray-haired riddle has recently modernized its old dress of "heredity" to DNA and genes. The riddle itself stubbornly survives.

While brave scientists hack a pathway into the unknown jungle of the human genetic code (the genome, a map showing how the cells work) a few giant truths hold their heads high. Here are two of them.

First, don't expect scientists to announce at a press conference that their research on DNA proves human beings are not responsible for their evil acts. Besides, a gang member will never convince a court judge by excusing his crime with "People don't kill, DNA does."

Second, although our environment influences or conditions our attitudes and behavior to some extent, we still remain master of our own decisions: we are free to choose our friends, our "hang-outs," our recreational reading, and especially the controls of our TV monster and cyberspace voyages.

In conclusion, nobody knows the exact answer to the vignette question but does it really matter as long as we recognize that we are influenced by both heredity and environment and remain responsible for our actions?

Discuss

A fourteen-year-old girl shouts to the judge, "I am not guilty of having killed that woman, my neighbor, because since I was four years old I had been abused sexually and emotionally by my mother's lovers."

CHAPTER 9

Where Am I? Was There Always A Universe?

"True science teaches, above all, to doubt."

Miguel De Unamuno

The Universe with No Spatial Boundaries	
Scientist	From ? to Big Bang
Uses empirical evidence	15 billion years ago
Philosopher	From Matter to Big Bang
Uses reason	Matter always existed
Theologian	From God to Matter to Big Bang
Uses faith in Bible	God created matter which led to Big Bang

Prologue

Student: Why must we always remember how scientists, philosophers, and believers think?

Teacher: So that we can differentiate problems that are scientific, philosophical, theological — religious — so that we can detect people in the media and in conversation who are confused in discussing these problems, so that we can avoid word salads.

The word "universe" encircles planet earth whirling away in its galaxy, (the Milky Way), together with all the other celestial bodies be they thick or thin, far or near.

To inquire whether the universe always existed is to ask whether some form of matter always existed from which the present universe somehow evolved. The composition of this original, very first matter, may have consisted of energy waves, gas, dust, and their combinations.

Performers

Student: Answer us, ye mighty astronomers, was there always a universe?

Astronomers: The universe burst into existence with a big bang about 15 billion years ago. By the big bang theory we mean that the universe began when all the matter then existing came together, collided, and exploded. The fireball expanded eventually into the billions of galaxies now populating the celestial sphere, which together with earth, we call the universe.

Philosopher: I notice how you astronomers accurately answered the students with an incomplete reply by remaining mute as to the age of matter before it blew up on big bang birthday. You carefully implied that your bag of empirical evidence — evidence derived from the senses — does not contain anything to qualify you to affirm anything prior to big bang day. In other words, astronomers cannot and are not expected to answer "Was there always a universe?" because Always is not a measurable term. This question is not phrased in scientific terms but in philosophical terms.

Student: By the way, how do you philosophers answer the question "Was there always a universe?" We just heard that the scientists or astronomers cannot answer it.

Philosopher: We answer that there is nothing unreasonable or illogical to assert that matter of some variety could have always existed — that matter never had a beginning — that it may always have existed, and in that sense matter would be eternal from its beginning.

Students: Having heard from astronomers and philosophers, let's ask theologians how they answer "Was there always a universe?"

Theologians: We modern Christian theologians echo Thomas Aquinas' answer — he was the most famous theologian of the Middle Ages — which may be paraphrased like this. "I know that the pagan Greek philosopher, Aristotle, is correct in saying that reason cannot disprove that the universe — some type of matter — may have always existed. However, we theologians possess another source of knowledge, a gift from God, called the virtue of faith, which tells us in the biblical book of Genesis that matter/universe did not always exist. It began when God created it.

Referee: To summarize — the scientist (astronomer) answers that the universe began more than 15 billion years ago. The philosopher speculates that matter may have always existed. The theologian — Jewish, Christian, and Muslim — replies that matter/universe did not always exist because God created it.

Notice how each of the three thinkers answers the question in accordance with his characteristic tool of acquiring knowledge: The scientist's tool is empirical evidence (with reason); the philosopher's tool is reason (supposing empirical evidence); the theologian's tool is faith in the biblical word.

Debate

Select three volunteers to represent scientists, philosophers, and theologians. How would each volunteer as a scientist, philosopher, or theologian answer this question: Could God have created eternal matter, i.e., could God have created the eternal particles of matter from which the big bang came? Have fun.

Exercises

1. Share any reading of science fiction relating to the big bang theory.
2. Comment on the epigraph.

CHAPTER 10

Will There Always Be A Universe? Candide By Voltaire

"Time is the image of eternity."

Diogenes Laertius

Ralph: I'm assuming that we are discussing whether there will always be a universe, not only planet earth.

Helen: We already know the answer about planet earth. For the first time in history we brilliant, but naughty, earthlings have the nuclear bombs ready to implode the planet and splatter its fizzling cinders off into space indefinitely.

Charles: So shall we reformulate our question this way? Will there always be some energy waves, gases, dust or combination thereof cruising in space just as they were before the big bang birthday?

Teacher: Excellent, Charles! To state a question clearly always fends off swarms of idle words. Let's turn over the question to our guest panelists.

Scientist: Empirical evidence does not permit me to predict the funeral date of the universe.

Adam: (Whispering to student Eva) He means that the scientists don't know

	when the last energy wave will whimper into extinction.
Eva:	(Slipping a written note) Thanks, Adam, but my intelligence got to me before your whisper.
Philosopher:	I submit that the last particles of matter, radio wave, other waves, etc., may continue forever, always, eternally, with no end. If matter never necessarily had a beginning, why would it necessarily have an end?
Theologian:	As a Christian theologian I answer from my Bible. "Tell us, they (the disciples ask Jesus) said, when will this (the destruction of the Jerusalem temple) happen? and what will be the signal for your coming and the end of the age?" Jesus continues, "And this gospel of the kingdom will be proclaimed throughout the earth as a testimony to all nations; and then the end will come," Matthew 24:3 and 14, RSV.
Teacher:	Observe once again that the scientist answers principally from empirical evidence, the philosopher from logic or reason, the theologian from faith in his Bible.

Discussion

1. Explain that the philosopher and the theologian not only disagree but contradict each other.

2. Why should the philosopher and the theologian nevertheless tolerate each

other's answer?

3. If you knew that planet earth would be destroyed in one month, what would you do during the month?

4. Comment on the epigraph.

Candide By Voltaire

A fiery debate raged in the European arena throughout the 1700s. From the German corner bounced a heavyweight named Leibnitz. He shouted, "All is for the best in the best of possible worlds." From the French corner sprang the challenger Voltaire, who screamed, "Nonsense! Read my novel, Candide."

The salons of Europe were chattering merrily about this sarcastic best seller. The following is a digest of Candide.

The scene opens at a baron's castle nestled in a German countryside. Cunegonde is the baron's daughter. Pangloss is the tutor of Cunegonde and also of Candide, a young male friend of the family.

One spring day as the stuffy baron strolls into the castle library, he surprises his daughter and Candide immersed in other than their books.

Expelled from the castle, the threesome, Pangloss, Cunegonde, and Candide venture on a world voyage. They stumble in and out of disasters as they travel — sometimes together, sometimes separately.

Throughout the voyage, Pangloss preaches that this is the best possible world and Candide objects that it is not.

Candide is conscripted into the Bulgarian army. He escapes to Holland where he overhears that Cunegonde was murdered. Candide and Pangloss wander to Lisbon, Portugal, where in this best possible world they arrive during the earthquake of 1755, on a Sunday morning when the churches are overflowing with worshippers.

Later the Inquisition condemns Candide and Pangloss. The latter is hanged, but Cunegonde (surprise!) looms up from nowhere to rescue Candide. He, in turn, murders the cardinal and the chief rabbi in the city at Cunegonde's establishment of ill-repute. In a panic after his double murder, Candide emerges safely in the Jesuit missions where a rebellion is heating up against the Spanish and Portuguese overlords. Candide continues on his murderous path as he kills the Jesuit general who just happens to be the brother of his sweetheart, Cunegonde. He decamps for El Dorado where he gathers a fortune in nuggets from the street gutters.

Upon his arrival in France, thieves relieve him of his wealth. Off he tramps to Portsmouth, England, and backtracks to Venice, Italy. He is stricken by the sad news that his darling was captured by pirates and is presently a washerwoman in Istanbul, Turkey. As Candide sails for Istanbul, he is amazed, while strolling on deck, to spot two galley slaves — Cunegonde's brother and Pangloss, neither of whom died after all.

When Candide finally rescues his beloved, he is shocked to behold how ugly she looks. Reluctantly, he marries her. In espousing her, Candide surrenders his hope for a better world and definitely rejects the teaching of Pangloss. Candide settles for an unhappy marriage in a stoic mood.

The satirical novel ends with all three laboring on a small farm. Pangloss still claims that all their evil misfortunes were for the best. Candide replies, with a statement henceforth repeated in world literature, "We must cultivate our garden," i.e., work is the answer to human unhappiness. The novel ends with the threesome living unhappily ever after in this best possible world.

Discussion

1. In the unending debate about the best possible world, do you favor the answer of Pangloss (that in spite of evils, it's the best possible world and, therefore, enjoy it)? Or do you favor the answer of Candide (that it's not the best possible world as daily evils, both personal and global demonstrate, but let's make the best of it)?
2. If you had been the grand architect at the dawn of creation, how would you have fashioned nature and human nature into a better world?
3. Write an essay, poem, play or short story on: Is This the Best Possible World?
4. Read Voltaire's Candide. Report three personal reflections about this novel.

CHAPTER 11

Can I Prove That God Exists? Why So Much Evil?

"If God did not exist, it would be necessary to invent him."

Voltaire

Prelude

Because one of America's experiments is to discover whether citizens of vastly different religious beliefs can live in harmony as one nation, would it not nourish the virtue of tolerance to ponder a few basic thoughts about God?

Teacher: Shall we whistle for our learned trio — the scientist, philosopher, theologian — to chew on this brainteaser?

Scientists

Scientist: We scientists lean heavily on sense evidence for valid knowledge. Please excuse us from the God search because "God" fails to meet the requirements for a scientific term. "God" is a word with which philosophers and theologians love to play. If compelled to answer, we will swivel our microscopes and telescopes on a material, god-like universal energy.

Fred: My mother read that some holy scientists were convinced at the end

	of their glorious careers that God exists.
Teacher:	True. When those scientists arrived at the God-conclusion, they were no longer lecturing in their capacity as scientists. They were speculating outside their field of science. They had cast off the science cap and pulled on a philosophy or theology cap. We'll now examine the wearers of the philosophy cap. How would philosophers — or anyone who reasons beyond sense evidence — sniff around the universe to detect whether God is hiding somewhere?

Philosophers

Philosopher:	Would I be correct in reasoning as follows? If I were jogging along the seashore and stumbled on a wristwatch — let's say I had never seen one before — my eyes would focus on the numerous complicated mechanisms whizzing in harmony to tell time. Now that the senses have offered their evidence of seeing, hearing, and feeling the wristwatch, my reason would click-in to conclude that because these mechanisms are too complex to have assembled by chance, therefore, there must have been a watchmaker. Did I reason logically to a watchmaker conclusion?
Chorus:	Yes!
Teacher:	Notice how the philosopher, doing what he does best, carefully

	unfolded the reasoning process when he concluded from the sense-knowledge of seeing, hearing, and feeling the wristwatch to a new nugget of knowledge — namely, the existence of a watchmaker.
Philosopher:	To continue — since my senses, especially my eyes peering at the stars through a telescope, focus my attention on billions of speeding celestial bodies, my reason snaps in to conclude, "Because these heavenly bodies are even more complex than mechanisms in a wristwatch, they could never have assembled by chance." My conclusion is that there must be a universe maker — God. What is illogical about my God-conclusion?
Chorus:	Nothing. Your conclusion sounds logical to us.
Philosopher:	Let's screw on the philosophy caps more tightly. Just because the complexity of a wristwatch leads us to the conclusion of a watchmaker, does it necessarily follow that the complexity of the universe must also lead us to the conclusion of a universe-maker-God?
Chorus:	Yes. Why not?
Philosopher:	Sorry. The answer is in the negative. Here's why. If required, we can verify our conclusion of a watchmaker by observing him at work. We cannot verify our conclusion of God building a universe by witnessing him constructing the universe. To summarize, we can

	prove the existence of a watchmaker from the evidence of a watch, but we cannot prove the existence of a universe-maker-God from the evidence of the universe. Spring this on a friend you want to impress — there is not one indisputable argument from reason to prove God's existence.
Ben:	So far we have inspected the answers of scientists and philosophers. It's time to inspect the answer of theologians or religious believers. How do they answer the riddle whether there is a God.

Theologians

Shirley:	Believers reply that God exists by pointing to relevant passages in the Bible.
Theologian:	Excellent answer, Shirley. Since the biblical God is a supernatural being, we cannot know "his" existence through reason. We accept his existence through the virtue of faith or trust on the authority of the Bible.
Arlene:	Before we dive into thicker clouds, what's the difference between an atheist and an agnostic?
Teacher:	An atheist is certain that there is no God. An agnostic is neutral. He is unwilling to affirm or deny the existence of God due to doubts. One celebrated agnostic, the British mathematician-philosopher, Bertrand Russell, is alleged to have been asked what he would reply

if, after his death, he met God. The Britisher replied, "Not enough evidence, My Lord."

Marie: (A recent émigré from England) A pox on scientists and philosophers. I don't care a tuppence for the grandiose conclusions of either of them. I'll continue to believe in God as my parents taught me.

God-Exercises

1. In your opinion, what evidence was Russell referring to? Evidence of the senses? Evidence of reason (proof by reasoning)? Neither? Discuss.

2. Would you perform evil acts if you became convinced that God does not exist? Why? Why not?

3. Comment in one page on the following statement of J. J. Rousseau, "I shall always maintain that whosoever says in his heart, 'there is no God,' while he takes the name of God upon his lips, is either a liar or a madman." (1)

4. The discussion above on God's existence was hammered out on the anvil of reason. Comment on Blaise Pascal's (1623-1662) oft-quoted dictum: "The heart knows something that the head is unaware of." (2)

5. Comment on the epigraph.

Why So Much Evil?

"Bad men live that they may eat and drink whereas good men eat and drink that they may live."

Socrates?

I'm Moral Evil	I'm Physical Evil

Alfred: I like nutshells. Could you give me a nutshell explanation of the problem of evil?

Teacher: Yes. If God is all-good and all-powerful, why does "He" allow evil?

Alfred: I was expecting a nutshell not a bombshell. We need a five minute recess to examine the bomb.

Voice: I'm a philosopher and my friend is a theologian. We can hear you from the corridor and hope that you would not mind if we assert that philosophers and theologians correctly distinguish between moral and physical evils.

Phyllis: Please give us some examples of moral evils.

Voice: Moral evils are unfair blows which human beings inflict upon one another, such as wars, murders, thefts, lies, character assassinations.

Yolanda: If God is all-good and all-powerful, why can't He/She stop these moral evils from striking innocent people?

Theologian: God allows us to operate our free will for good or evil while we are living on this earth. We will be punished for our evil acts or rewarded for our good acts after death in the next life.

Bernard: Having clarified why moral evils snake the world over, give us examples of physical evils.

Philosopher: Here is a plateful — floods, hurricanes, earthquakes, diseases, and other disasters spawned by Mother Nature.

Emily: If God is so powerful and good and there is no question of free will in these calamities of Mother Nature, why can't God prevent them? Or, at least diminish the power of their destructive punches?

Theologian: Since Alfred likes nutshell answers, let's be candid. Whether we are Jewish, Christian or Muslim theologians, we cannot adequately answer why God does not restrain the vandal hand of Mother Nature. It's a mystery.

Bertha: Whenever a tornado swoops down, my grandmother says that God is punishing us.

Theologian: With all due respect to grandmother, if God punishes some people with a tornado and not others, God would be unjust.

Bertha: Sounds logical and theological to me, but not to my grandmother.

Ram: I'm a Hindu. We Hindus and Buddhists teach that the belief in one God is only a stepping-stone to the belief that everything is "God." Westerners call us pantheists. Therefore we are not troubled by the

	problem of evil. The belief in one "God" is a hang-up in the Western world.
Teacher:	In summary, we defined and gave examples of moral and physical evils. Moral evils depend on free will. Theologians cannot adequately answer why an all-good and all-powerful God cannot prevent physical evils.
Philosopher:	If you believe something vehemently you can always give an answer even if it is an inadequate one.

Evil Exercises

1. I don't believe in God because if there were a God how could He/She have allowed the evils of World War I and II, the Korean War, The Vietnam War, and the two Gulf wars?

2. The Buddhists suffer from moral and physical evils like the rest of mankind. So, how do they get away with not answering the problem of evil?

3. If God is all-wise and all-powerful, why can't He/She make a square circle?

4. If God is all-wise and all-powerful, why can't He/She stop an irresistible force from displacing an immovable object?

5. What do you think is the greatest flaw in nature? Storms? What?

6. What do you think is the greatest flaw in human nature? Pride? Greed? What?

7. Chew on the following speculation by the unknown philosopher: My guess

for a solution to the problem of physical evil is that it is of the very nature or essence of matter that there must be natural catastrophes such as storms, floods, earthquakes. Matter cannot be matter unless it contains these activities.

8. Comment on the epigraph.

CHAPTER 12

**What Is The Best Type Of Government And For Whom?
Monarchy, Dictatorship, Democracy.
Socialists vs. Capitalists**

Citizen: Why am I interested in this question? Because I want to know whether I should feel more proud about my country's exportation of democracy than I am of its exportation of movies, popular music, jeans, and fast foods.

Monarchy

"Now when the ruin sets in, where does it regularly make its first appearance? In kings or in the common people?"

Plato

Queen of England: Since I won the contest of the royals, I'll speak for the other queens and kings of Norway, Sweden, Denmark, the Netherlands, Belgium, etc. We usually inherit the throne. Hardly any monarch actually exercises genuine political power. We wield a symbolic power as figureheads of the nation.

Queen of Denmark: Since I won second prize, I have a right to talk. Let's be frank. We of the royal heap are first class P. R. professionals who parade in pomp and circumstance on festive occasions before the masses and

	thereby hope to keep the people obedient to our government officials.
King of Belgium:	Since I won third place, I would like to crown these remarks thus — some rulers call themselves kings, but they are only dictators in royal robes. We royals will now bow out and from the pinnacle of our thrones, we'll lend an ear to the discussion between dictators and "democrats" who truly exercise power.

Dictatorship

"Whenever law ends tyranny begins."

John Locke

Asian dictator:	A dictatorship is a type of government by which one person alone rules the nation. A dictator is not elected by the people but is often carried to power on the shoulders of the military. You may know some dictators of past history — Cyrus, Alexander the Great, Caesar, Napoleon.
African dictator:	We dictators may preside over a council that votes laws for the country but everyone knows the council is window dressing. In fact, some dictators proclaim their governments to be republics.
Teacher:	There are several countries in West Africa, which are not even ruled by dictators, but by rival warlords.

Democracy

"Democracy, which is a charming form of government, full of variety and disorder, dispenses a sort of equality to equals and unequals alike."

Plato

U. S. President: We Americans boast about being the number one democratic country in the world. Our foreign policy is energized by sowing democracy all over the planet.

Stacey: Mr. President, we are taught to always begin a discussion by defining our terms. Please define democracy.

President: A democracy is a type of government by which the people themselves rule their own country. This is a common denominator definition of democracy and also its root meaning from the Greek, demos, meaning "people," and kratein, meaning "to rule." Besides this general definition, there is a strict definition according to which the people themselves freely debate and finally agree by majority vote on their own laws, penalties, and procedures in the governing of their country.

Historian: Two historical examples of a democracy in the strict sense take us to fifth century B. C. Athens and to 17th century New England town hall meetings. A contemporary American class of examples of democracy in the strict sense is the occasional state or local referendum.

Janet: Is there any country in the world today that is a democracy in the strict sense?

Historian: No, Janet. Jean Jacques Rousseau, a philosopher who died in 1778, already answered your question when he wrote that strictly speaking a democracy has never existed and never will. A democracy in the contemporary world is a representative democracy commonly called a republic.

Fred: Name some.

Historian: Japan, Canada, Latin American countries, and European countries. But to continue, in a republic, the people elect representatives to formulate policies, laws, and penalties. The representatives allegedly govern for the benefit of the people whose wishes they are elected to represent.

Hilda: My father says that representatives fill their pockets and fill those of special interest groups, the wealthy upper crust of society, and the giant bulldog corporations.

Sidney: My father says that the representatives are bought by the lobbyists and that lobbying is legalized bribery. There are no lobbyists for the poor, the homeless, and the uninsured because they have no money to hire lobbyists. Call that democracy of the people?

President: We are not perfect. We like to boast that no country is more

	democratic than ours.
Isaac:	Since some republics are more democratic than others, they enjoy more freedoms and rights in self-government. What are the steps, which a baby democracy takes on its journey to become a mature adult democratic nation? Or, what are the degrees of democracy?
Professor:	The first step taken by an infant democratic nation is a free election. There are many intermediate steps between free election all the way to a bill of rights — or constitution — if there is one. This quantum leap may take only a brief period as in the 13 American colonies or it may take a long time as in some present-day South American countries. The reason why the democracy of a newborn nation grows rapidly or slowly depends on whether its people had or had not previously enjoyed a tradition of at least some political freedoms and consensus-making. In the 13 original American colonies, democracy grew rapidly because the colonists had previously practiced some political freedoms in Europe. On the other hand, democracy in present-day Russia will mature very slowly because its people have lived under dictatorships for centuries and had never lived under a democracy.
Asian Statesman:	I've been snooping via satellite as you smug westerners — North Americans and Europeans — chat away, high and mighty, as if there

is only one brand of democracy. Allow me to explode your honorable myth by acquainting you with a common view of democracy in the Eastern countries of the globe. It's simply this. In your practice of democracy you value the rights of the individual over those of the community. We reverse the values. We value the rights of the community over those of the individual. As individuals, we willingly and voluntarily surrender our individual preferences, if in so doing the community, not the dictator and his clique, benefits. For example, if the United States Government makes a law that would benefit the majority of the people, up to 95%, but it would conflict with the rights of the 5%, your ethicians would call the law immoral because the rights of some individuals would be violated. On the other hand, we in the East would laugh up our sleeves. Why? Because, if the same law were passed in China, Malaysia, etc., the 5% would yield voluntarily to the 95% for the simple reason that the community comes first. We think as a nation, not as an individual against the nation. That community mentality has been in our Asian tradition for millennia and it's expressed in our lives, laws, arts, and literature. The results of a community mentality are obvious in our family values, which are far superior to yours as is apparent in your abuse of guns, drugs, and broken families. I realize that it's difficult for you westerners to understand and accept our practice of democracy. At the very least you could air our view in your high schools, colleges, and universities. Have a nice day.

Two Economic Systems

Socialism and capitalism are rival economic systems. Since democratic countries are fueled by capitalism, it's easy to confuse capitalism with democracy.

Socialists

Ghost of Karl Marx: The slogan of socialists is: Everyone works according to his ability and receives according to his needs. The slogan is finely tuned to picture an ideal family working together. We socialists favor the government ownership of the principal means of production. We promote a command economy by which the workers make products according to a schedule dictated by the government. This command type of socialism was practiced by us in the former Soviet Union in Russia and throughout its communist empire before it collapsed.

Two dictators: We are the dictators and we are proud to say that we have not collapsed. We are still communist countries with command economies.

Ghost of Lenin: When I was the dictator of Russia, we socialists bragged that from the rich soil of socialism there would eventually blossom the flower

|||of communism when everything will be owned by its citizens and not by the government.
Historian: | Such a utopian communistic nation, large or small, has never blossomed neither in ancient nor in modern times. Admittedly, random religious groups have realized communal, "communistic" living.
Socialist critic: | Back to the question of socialism. The shrieking cracks in a socialist command economy are the workers' lack of initiative and excessive, mindless dependence on the government. To illustrate, it suffices to contrast the anemic energy of the former East German communist workers with the robust energy of West German capitalist workers.
Norwegian: | In present-day socialist countries, e.g., Norway and Sweden, our citizens willingly pay heavy taxes in return for welfare programs, especially health care, and comfortable retirement benefits.

Capitalists

Political scientist: | Capitalism is characterized by "free enterprise" because it struggles to compete freely for profits with rivals to make the best product for consumers to buy.
Critic: | However, since greed is the homegrown disease of many capitalists, as evidenced by false advertisements, shabby products, overpricing, price fixing, immoral CEOs, and cost effectiveness instead of human

	safety, the government is obligated to protect its citizens by regulations and prosecution of hoggish companies.
Frieda:	My mother has a degree in economics. She preaches that most citizens of capitalist countries are unaware of how many socialist ingredients are mixed in the capitalist soup. Agree?
Political scientist:	Yes. Mother hit the bull's-eye. In capitalist America, some of its socialist ingredients are social security, welfare programs for the poor — frequently mentioned in the press — welfare programs for corporations — infrequently mentioned in the press — government bailouts of big business, such as the Chrysler Corporation and the savings and loans associations.
Abraham:	My uncle is an editor. He insists that both socialists and capitalists are riddled with vices.
Political scientist:	That's why no major country is 100% socialist or capitalist. Most European countries are capitalist, heavily dosed with socialistic elements. The ideal economic system would consist of the proper brew of both socialism and capitalism. No economist or political scientist has yet prescribed the perfect recipe.
Teacher:	To summarize, we defined three types of government — monarchy, dictatorship, and democracy — and two types of economic systems — socialism and capitalism.

Steve: Why have you purposely delayed answering the last part of the question in the title, "What is the best type of government and for whom?"

Teacher: The best type of government for a country with total or near total literacy is democracy. Democracy thrives best when the citizenry is educated, involved, and experienced in working together. The best type of government for a nation of total or near-total illiterates is a benign dictator, if one can be located, until the citizens are coached to initiate the democratic process by freely electing a ruler.

Democratic Exercises

1. Debate which country is more democratic; England or America. (Take note that England has no constitution.)

2. Critique the idea of democracy by the Asian statesman quoted above. Is he talking about a legitimate form of democracy? (1)

3. Aristotle taught that he who has no need of a society because he is self-sufficient, must be either a beast or a god. Give three examples why it's necessary to live in society if this is your opinion.

4. Show how you can reconcile or how you cannot reconcile the two following viewpoints:

    a) "... government of the people, by the people, and for the people ..." (*Gettysburg Address by Abraham Lincoln*).

b) There are no poor people in America who need government assistance. Their numbers are exaggerated by liberals. Besides, there are millions of welfare cheaters; there are those who choose not to work and, therefore, don't deserve assistance; there are those who choose to remain poor and sleep under bridges or on warm sidewalk grates; there are timid, unmotivated souls who need a boot and told to get a job and become self-reliant in the good old American spirit. The poor we will always have with us.

5. Are you for or against the form of government envisioned for America by the Project for the New American Century? (2)

6. Since 9/11 a controversy has been stewing about where to draw the line between protection against terrorists and the curtailment of traditional American civil liberties. The nerve center of the controversy is whether the government is using the fight against terrorism as an excuse to chip away at American liberties. What is your opinion?

7. Would you conclude from J. J. Rousseau's statement above (Historian's answer to Janet) that he shows a high or low regard for the fifth century B. C. Athenian democracy?

8. Comment on each of the three epigraphs.

9. A cooperative class project in group learning:

a) Students separate into six groups.

b) Teacher assigns to each group one of the following six core values common to a democratic society: Fairness, Respect, Citizenship, Responsibility, Trustworthiness, and Caring. (3)

c) Each group selects its own recording secretary.

d) Each group agrees on a definition of the core value assigned to it. (15 minutes)

e) Each group agrees on three examples illustrating its core value. (25 minutes)

f) After each group has agreed upon the definition of its core value and three examples, the six recording secretaries report their summaries to the reassembled class.

g) All students cast a secret "objective" ballot as to which group through its recording secretary report gave the best definition and the best three examples.

h) The victorious group receives a prize (e.g., no homework for one week).

i) The teacher may request that the winning report be printed in the school paper.

ETHICAL WARM-UP

CHAPTER 13

May I Go On A Civil Disobedience Spree?

"Good laws lead to the making of better ones: bad ones bring about worse."

J. J. Rousseau

Definition

Civil disobedience is a "refusal to obey the demands or commands of the government especially as a non-violent collective means of forcing concessions from the government," (Webster's Dictionary).

Seven Conditions

Civil disobedience may be morally justified if seven conditions are fulfilled:

1. The issue must be a major, moral issue (building a nuclear plant) and often a political issue (sanctions against a foreign country).

2. The decision to disobey must be reached in accordance with the dictates of one's informed conscience.

3. The demonstration must benefit the public good not an individual or a particular group.

4. The demonstration must be discharged by a group and in public view. It must not be a private grudge as were those of the "Unabomber" and of Timothy McVeigh's bombing of the Oklahoma City Federal building.

5. The demonstration must be nonviolent.

6. The disobedience must be a last resort. All other non-disobedient attempts were tried and failed.

7. The participants must willingly accept the penalty. (1)

Discussion Spree

1. Apply the seven conditions to the following examples in order to decide whether the examples are justifiable cases for civil disobedience:
    a) Protests outside abortion clinics
    b) Protests against the World Trade Organization, the International Monetary Fund or the World Bank

2. Find a newspaper or magazine account of a civil disobedience. Are any of the seven conditions present? Absent?

3. Would you prefer to eliminate any of the seven conditions as unnecessary? Why?

4. Would you prefer to add one or more to the seven conditions? List and explain them. (2)

5. Comment on the epigraph.

CHAPTER 14

Can I Be A Patriot And A Cosmopolitan Citizen?

"I am not an Athenian or a Greek but a citizen of the world."

Socrates ?

Reveille for a Book Review

One of America's most respected philosophers, Martha C. Nussbaum, has written an exciting, controversial book on patriotism. (1) We will summarize her thesis and scan 16 critical replies included in the same book. Afterwards, fully armed, we'll jump into a skirmish discussion.

Dr. Nussbaum defends her position that we can be citizens of the world, cosmopolitans. This stance, she stoutly maintains, should be incorporated within the American civic educational system. (p. 11)

Her trumpet does not summon us to divide our allegiance, our loyalty, between America and the world. Some of her critics may interpret her in this vein but I do not. It's understandable that we Americans should devote more time and study to the history and institutions of our own nation. (p. 13)

As a reminder that cosmopolitanism is not an original doctrine, the author points to the Greco-Roman, Stoic philosophers' teachings on being citizens of the world. In addition she exemplifies cosmopolitanism in a modern setting with frequent references to a novel by

Rabindranah Tagore entitled The Home and The World. (2) The novel illustrates how one can be both a patriot of one's country and a patriot of the world.

Nussbaum emphasizes that we Americans must look beyond our borders whenever we examine our national problems. Regardless of the problem, be it pollution, racism, crime, poverty, we must view our national concerns through international binoculars. She means that we should at least "imagine" how other countries inspect the same issue. If we forget to put on our international spectacles we will fall into the trap of assuming that our national solution is the normal one (p. 12), the one-size solution that fits all nations. To paraphrase the author's thought, we would be barking to the world audience, "America is the measure of all nations."

We ought to realize that the values called rights, democracy, justice, liberty, all beings are created equal with certain inalienable rights (p. 13) are also the legitimate yearnings of all other nationals. This empathy is an important ingredient of being a citizen of the world. As a bonus, we may solve our nation's woes more efficiently if we view them as citizens of the cosmos.

Several of the 16 critics admire Dr. Nussbaum for carrying the banner of cosmopolitanism alone into the academic battle. She realizes that patriotism is comfortable and that cosmopolitanism is "often a lonely business." (p. 15) Many of her critics sling arrows by quoting some of her phrases out of context. Various critics reply to Dr. Nussbaum's thesis in vague, general terms to which she replies in kind.

Patriotic-Cosmopolitan Discussion

1. What is the first image that splashes on your imagination screen when you hear the word "patriot"?

2. Do you consider yourself a "patriot"? If yes, explain why; if no, explain why not?

3. In your opinion, would you say that the American school children who contributed money to buy back Sudanese children from the northern Sudanese slave traders was a patriotic act? A cosmopolitan act? Both? Neither? All of the above? Explain.

4. According to Dr. Nussbaum, how would a cosmopolitan spirit make a stronger American patriotic spirit?

5. Dr. Nussbaum asks why the Chinese living in the United Sates are "our fellows" (p. 14), but were not when they previously lived in China. Explain.

6. Apparently, Dr. Nussbaum speaks of two different aspects of cosmopolitanism: one aspect consists in imagining how a national program would be handled by a foreign nation; a second aspect, "we need knowledge not only of the geography and ecology of other nations . . . but also a great deal about the people" (p. 12). Does either aspect appeal to you? Why? Why not?

7. Would you consider a CEO, who legally defrauded his employees (by cooking the books) from their investments and pension funds, to be a

patriot? Explain.

8. Could an American who has no interest in the problems of other Americans be a cosmopolitan? Explain.

9. Because all the peoples of the world are coming closer to one another in a global village due to the information age, and due to our common problems of pollution, trade disputes, etc., could all this help us become cosmopolitan in outlook? Explain.

10. Would an American strutting around the global village with a chip on his shoulder "My country right or wrong" be a patriot? A cosmopolitan? Both? Neither? Explain.

11. Is an American cosmopolitan a traitor of his countrymen or a model for his countrymen? Explain.

12. Gore Vidal writes that American administrations for decades have been changing the United States into an empire. The empire is not acquired in the old-fashioned way by raising a flag over a conquered country and by taking over its land. The empire is acquired in a modern way by global military presence and by international financial control. NATO is one way to control Europe; Japan serves as a base in the Far Eastern theater; the CIA is used for clandestine activities even in interfering with national elections abroad; wars are declared when needed mostly without the approval of the American people nor of congress. Simultaneously Americans find themselves with less

and less constitutional rights. (3) Would you evaluate Gore Vidal as a patriot? A cosmopolitan? A traitor? A rare American exercising his constitutional rights, fearless of his government and of the national press?

13. Comment on the epigraph.

CHAPTER 15

Why Can't Church And State Get Along?

"To go to Canossa" (1)

Vatican City

Pope: Since you international dignitaries requested me to host this summit meeting in sunny Italy, I will not participate in the discussion. A glance at the round table suffices to indicate that the relationship between government and religion differs in each country.

Archbishop of Canterbury: In England Anglicanism is the state religion.

Finish dignitary: Finland recognizes two state religions — the Lutheran and the Greek Orthodox.

U. S. Supreme Court Judge: On the other side of the ocean the U. S. Government recognizes no state religion and would fight tooth and nail against such a marriage. In fact, America rejoices about a separation of church and state. This separation was the verdict after bitter infighting among the original 13 colonies.

Gore Vidal (telephone call): Contrary to a prevalent myth in American history textbooks, the Puritans did not flock to American shores to flee from religious persecutions in Europe but to freely persecute other religions.

U. S. Supreme Court Judge: The American policy of the separation of church and state is engraved in the first amendment of the Bill of Rights: "Congress shall make no law respecting an establishment of religion or prohibiting the free exercise thereof." The principle is clear but its application is unclear.

Swiss dignitary: I have closely followed the news about the conflicts between church and state in America. I have yet to smoke out whether there is any basic interpretation prevalent in the courts, congress, and the news media.

U. S. Supreme Court Judge: There are two basic interpretations, which even most Americans are not aware of. One interpretation says no aid. The government must help neither religious nor secular organizations. The opposing interpretation says that if the government decides to help, it must help equally all religious and secular organizations. Here is an example. The Supreme Court, five to four, in 1995, granted Wide Awake, a Christian student publication of the Virginia State University, equal funding as it did to the secular publications of the same university. (2) Other examples of government aid refer to social programs like drug treatment, nursing homes, homeless shelters, childcare centers, funds for elementary and secondary education, colleges, and universities.

German Lutheran dignitary: We Germans began the great separation between church and state, which is known as the Reformation. I keep an attentive ear to your conflicts. Some are trivial and some are serious. I predict that your church-state conflicts will persist to the last breath of the American Republic.

Russian Greek Orthodox Archbishop: Most of the European countries of the Greek Orthodox persuasion get along rather well with our governments, like Slovenia, Serbia, Slovakia, Bulgaria. Why all this church tension in America? Don't you have enough squabbles already?

American historian: We are battered with all these church discords because the principle of the separation is difficult to apply. In spite of it, America is known as a religious country in beliefs and practices, even though some nickname us "the evil empire."

American Fundamentalist representative: I agree with the archbishop that we engage in scuffles and they will increase. To the historian I reply that we have a secular reputation, which is due to the practice of treating religion as unimportant, as a private affair not even to be elevated to the level of polite conversation. The government for years has cast religion aside in public life, in business, in the press, and especially in the schools. Consequently many of us concluded that if we sit idly by and watch the secular parade, soon the entire nation will be stripped of its

Judeo-Christian heritage and religious values. This galloping secularization provoked us to demand more influence in national life and more financial aid.

American church sociologist: The friction between church and state is further heated by at least two antagonisms. First, the churches themselves eye one another with unease if the government appears to favor one of them. For example, the Bush administration is accused of partiality towards the beliefs of the fundamentalist churches. (3) Second, the Americans United for the Separation of Church and State pose as watch-dogs, ready to sound the alarm when either the church or the state tries to undermine the wall of separation.

American Supreme Court Judge: In all these troubled waters the Ship of State has granted its various religious practitioners standard exemptions. Two popular ones are tax exemptions — income taxes and property taxes with qualifications — and military service exemption. Chaplains are expected to enlist as needed. Other exemptions and rights refer to fair labor law obligations; eligibility public office; educational standards. (4) Some church/state disputes that made headlines in the past are: the Reverend Sun Myung Moon who appealed his conviction of tax fraud, (5), scientology, Hare Krishna, (6) , Bob Jones University. (7)

Uninvited philosopher's email: May I submit the following guidelines to church/state disputants as they continue their tip-toeing through the mine fields of a separate but mutually suspicious coexistence? First, the relationship between church and state works best when untested — when the clergy remains behind its church walls and does nothing to test the legal waters of separation. Second, no tax-exempt church should engage in any competitive business. If any church officials dare to enter the jungle of the business world, they should obtain a license and pay taxes. Third, church buildings sometimes occupy valuable land. The land would earn high taxes for the local community if owned by civilians. The religious officials of such buildings should utilize them to full capacity not minimal capacity just to avoid taxes. Fourth, sooner or later the churches will have to pay taxes. Therefore, they should tread cautiously in all areas of business.

American Liberal Protestant: It's fitting to review some church players and their burning issues. The abortion issue is the front-runner of all the bickering between church and state. In opposition to us Liberal Protestants there are the three Protestant Fundamentalist groups — the Evangelical Conservatives, part of which is the Southern Baptist Convention with 16 million members; the Holiness churches; the Pentecostal-Charismatic churches. Some of their fiery issues are school prayer, the teaching of creationism in public schools, (see chap. 4). (8)

Discussion

1. Share with your peers whatever comes to mind when you hear "church and state."

2. Have you ever heard of "church and state" in any of your courses? Which courses?

3. In your opinion, is it a violation of the separation of church and state to have money inscribed with "in God we trust"? Explain.

4. Can you think of any particular religion, which is attempting to influence the government? Explain.

5. Would you object if Congress changed the Bill of Rights and declared one religion as the state religion? Explain.

6. In your opinion, who causes more trouble, the government or the churches?

7. Do you think that it would be a violation of the separation of church and state if a Christian cross were planted on public property? Why?

8. If the President consulted you, which of the two guidelines — as explained by the U. S. Supreme Court Judge — would you propose for a smoother relationship between church and state? Why?

9. In your opinion, which would constitute a more serious violation of the separation of church and state: a) an American judge who decorates the state

capitol with a marble slab of the Ten Commandments or b) an American President who exerts his political power to advance his religious beliefs?

10. Comment on the epigraph.

CHAPTER 16

Has The State The Right To Inflict The Death Penalty? Debate Rules

"Revenge is a kind of wild justice, which the more man's nature runs to, the more ought law to weed it out."

Francis Bacon

NEWSFLASH

Since numerous Europeans register dismay at the popular American adoption of the death penalty, we decided to stage a debate in Iceland during the winter to discourage uninvited protesters from firing iceballs at the convention center.

Debate Master: Hear Ye! Hear Ye! These are the debate rules. First, this will be a scholarly debate not a TV or radio free-for-all. Therefore no jokes, insults, sarcasms, anecdotes or off-the-subject remarks will be tolerated.

Second, an important assumption of the debate is that a government imposes a punishment — death penalty, imprisonment, fines, whatever — in order to prevent the victim's loved ones from seeking revenge, from taking the law into their own hands, from disrupting law and order in society. Incidentally, the young logicians in the gallery know that an assumption is a statement, which is not discussed because it's taken for granted.

Third, this debate will not be like the death penalty controversy screeching across American newspapers: "Should Death Row Inmates Receive the Death Penalty?" It's common knowledge that at least some death row prisoners are innocent even though a court branded them guilty. The court appointed lawyer for the low-income prisoners may have been ill prepared; the judge may have forbidden crucial evidence due to a legal technicality; witnesses may have erred or been bribed; an eloquently gifted prosecutor may have duped a gullible jury. The precise issue of the debate is: Should a proven guilty murderer receive the death penalty? The operative word is proven and not only proven "beyond a reasonable doubt." The doubt may be tainted with one or more of the defects listed above. The proof must be beyond any doubt whatsoever like Jack Ruby who shot Lee Harvey Oswald, the assassin of President John F. Kennedy, in plain view of a nationwide television audience. Mr. America defends the affirmative position. Mr. Europe the negative. You go first Mr. America.

Mr. America: A proven guilty murderer should receive the death penalty because it is a legal form of punishment in many of our states in democratic America.

Debate Master: Overruled. The debate is concerned with the morality of the death

	penalty law itself. In other words, is the death penalty law itself moral? Try again Mr. America.
Mr. America:	The death penalty law is moral because it protects society against a particular individual murderer. He or she will never murder again.
Mr. Europe:	I counter with the principal refutation of the death penalty by replying that life imprisonment will protect society equally well as the death penalty.
Debate Master:	Since Mr. America does not rebut, Mr. Europe has scored one point. Proceed.
Mr. America:	The death penalty is moral because it's a deterrent — a lesson for others.
Mr. Europe:	Deterrence has never been proven to serve as an effective lesson against crime.
Debate Master:	Since Mr. America does not reply, Mr. Europe has scored a second point. You may proceed with a third thrust, Mr. America.
Mr. America:	The death penalty is a moral punishment because it's in accordance with the virtue of justice. I'll explain how justice works in the death penalty controversy. When a person is proven to have deliberately and with complete forethought taken an innocent life, that murderer, in all justice, forfeits his or her life for the life taken.
Mr. Europe:	I refute your definition of justice by describing what it really is and

	then by qualifying justice. I describe your justice as too strict and as nothing but the law of retaliation, of an eye for an eye justice, of revenge, of vendetta. I qualify justice. Justice must be balanced with mercy to be an effective law in society. For this qualification I offer three arguments. First, no parents have ever ruled a happy family by strict justice.
Debate Master:	Excuse me Mr. Europe. You young logicians in the gallery should note Mr. Europe's first argument. It is really only a comparison. A comparison is the weakest form of argument. However, occasionally comparisons have some proving value as does Mr. Europe's family comparison. Most comparisons do not. Please continue.
Mr. Europe:	Second, no government in history has ever succeeded in governing a happy people by the law of strict justice. Third, nations, even nowadays, who retaliate according to strict justice have yet to reach a cease-fire.
Debate Master:	Since Mr. America declines to comment, Mr. Europe scores a third point and we will end the debate. Mr. Europe is the winner with three points. And, I would also like to announce another winner — the Icelandic chief-of-police whose leadership prevented the uninvited protesters' iceballs from breaking any windows of our newly restored convention center.

Unknown philosopher: Not a word was spoken in favor of restitution to the victims' loved ones. They often suffer emotionally, physically, and financially. That's a glaring flaw in the justice system. That's my opinion but whoever asks me for my opinion?

Debate Master: It's customary to end debates with a light remark from the sergeant at arms.

Sergeant at arms: Last summer as our tour bus hobbled past the courthouse in Cuzco, Peru, the guide pointed to the inscription on the portals: Palacio de Justicia — palace of justice. He humored us, "We Cuzco citizens say, 'too much palace and not enough justice.'"

Discussion
by those who missed their plane to Iceland

1. To which debater would you say that the following observation made by an American tourist in Italy is most applicable? "More than one Italian courthouse had inscribed on its portals: GIUSTIZIA E GRAZIA (Justice and Mercy)."

2. Comment on the opinion of the unknown philosopher. How, in your opinion, could the guilty person compensate the victim's loved ones?

3. Rewrite the debate so that your opinion will win.

4. Rewrite the debate so that those opposed to the death penalty, because of their religious beliefs, will win.

5. Comment on the epigraph.

Debate Rules

Gaze in disbelief at how TV moderators and panelists sin against common rules of logic.

If you saw the same TV moderators for several months you probably mused to yourself, "How can one person be well informed on every topic of science, economics, history, law, politics, world events, and so on?" You correctly concluded that he could not, regardless of the prepared researched questions stuffed into his hands.

Moderators are not experts. They stroll into snares with the greatest of ease. For example, they will not always detect fallacies, irrelevant remarks, and rambling anecdotes.

In an ideal logical discussion the moderator presides as an expert on the topic. You would expect that a TV moderator at least should be sharp enough to enforce a handful of rudimentary rules some of which are the following:

First Rule

Be specific. In a logical discussion, a moderator, like a referee, should insist that the panelists agree on a specific topic and not on a general free-for-all topic. The moderator should explain what's presumed and what's excluded. For instance, the topic may be "Should the welfare program be administered by Washington or by individual states?" What's presumed? We all want the money to go to those who really need it. What's excluded? — all slurs about the politicians in the nation's capital and in the state capitals.

Second Rule

No meandering. Moderators, like traffic cops, should gently but firmly direct the wandering panelists back to the topic. The media moderators are at fault when they themselves wander by sandwiching unrelated, dramatically charged questions into the discussion in order to boost ratings. They are also deficient when they bait two panelists into a verbal duel to heighten sensationalism instead of illumination.

Third Rule

Continue a disagreement to the end. Moderators should guide the discussion to a solution or at least to a conclusion. Here lies the most distressing flaw of media debates. Moderators often interrupt, "we're running out of time so let's go to the next question." The moderator should never go to the next question until a particular point under discussion is resolved. If panelist Blake is delivering a red-hot refutation to panelist Drake, the moderator ought to allow Blake to complete his refutation. A skillful moderator will not allow Drake to change the subject or deliver an ad hominem (below the belt blow) but the moderator should encourage Drake to either rebut the refutation or admit defeat. Only after this conclusion may the moderator go to the next question. The homespun axiom of former President Truman springs to mind, "If you don't like the heat, stay out of the kitchen." Permit a copycat, "If you don't like the refutation stay out of the disputation."

Fourth Rule

This rule is for the panelists. Less conceit, please. A gloomy question raises its head.

How do you explain that panelists-experts are not more logical? The frank answer is that they are often prejudiced in favor of their own opinions. In their thinking there are only two opinions — theirs and the wrong one. This conceited mentality easily leads them to the favorite, juicy fallacy of remarks made to the man instead of to his reasons.

Fifth Rule

Admit to a K. O. punch. A panelist should admit when refuted fairly and squarely by a fellow panelist. Panelists labor under a wicked belief that an admission of refutation equates an admission of public humiliation. Not so. Such an admission signifies self-confidence. The admission signals that one is big enough to acknowledge an error. Instead of being pitied he would be admired for intellectual honesty. In final analysis, the purpose of a dispute is to seek light not glory.

An historical example: President Kennedy's public admission of his error in the failed Bay of Pigs invasion of Cuba. His admission shut off a tidal wave of criticism. The President's stature was not diminished but increased. Kennedy was confident enough to broadcast his error of judgment.

Field Work

1. What rules would you add to the five above?
2. Were any of the five rules violated in the death penalty debate above?
3. Write or report orally about a TV discussion you watched. What was the topic?

4. Was the topic clearly defined? Critique the moderator. Critique the panelists.

5. Compose a debate from whole cloth about a topic that enormously consumes your interest. Show how you apply one or more of the five rules above.

6. Comment on each of the five rules.

CHAPTER 17

Is It Ethical To Punish Human Beings?

"In nature there are neither rewards nor punishments — there are only consequences."

R. G. Ingersoll (1)

An Imaginary Trialogue on Devil's Island

| John Stuart Mill | The Attorney General | Osama bin Laden |

Prison Warden: Thank you for selecting Devil's Island, the former penal colony, in pleasant French Guiana, South America. Allow me to introduce the three panelists of this worldwide televised trialogue. John Stuart Mill (who died in 1873) was an English philosopher renowned for the utilitarian theory of ethics. The attorney general of the United States needs no introduction. Osama bin Laden, associated with the twin towers disaster of 9/11/2001 is unfortunately too well known. The focus of today's topic is on a wider ethical question than capital punishment. It asks whether the punishment of human beings is ethically justifiable, that is, whether it's ethically justifiable to punish adults who commit a serious crime, murder, theft, etc. The panelists will not discuss the punishment of children by parents nor whether teens should be put on trial and punished as adults.

Attorney General: I answer with an unequivocal yes in the name of the retribution (giving back) theory. Offenders must be punished. The reason is that they committed a crime. The punishment is what they give back to the community for the crime committed. A clear example of the retributive theory is the law of retaliation often expressed as "an eye for an eye." Unfortunately, this theory has dominated the Palestine-Israeli conflict. A common saying also illustrates the retribution theory — "let the punishment fit the crime."

J. S. Mill: I also answer in the affirmative. Yes, it is ethical to punish adult criminals but only on the condition that the punishment will result in some good, like the protection of the criminals themselves from committing further crimes or like setting an example to would-be criminals. If these "goods" do not result from the punishment or if they do not prevent evil acts from happening again, the punishment would be unethical, unjustifiable. The word *utilitarian* in my theory means that the punishment must be "useful," i.e., good useful results must outweigh the evil results of punishment. That's why we utilitarians are recognized by our slogan — "the greatest good for the greatest number" (of people). (2)

Osama bin Laden: Besides the theory of retribution and that of utility there is another theory which is much more popular, the theory of revenge. That's my style. It's only human to experience feelings of hate, revenge, and the pleasure from revenge.

Psychologist's email: The issue here is not that victims and their dear ones do not instinctively feel anger and desires for revenge but the issue is what do they do with these feelings? Do they gradually shrug them off and forgive? Or do they use them for revenge and wallow in them? I might as well continue. I object to the utilitarian theory by claiming that hardened criminals must be punished even if the punishment does not result in some good because: hardened criminals frequently come from failed marriages; they purposely join criminal gangs in order to acquire a feeling of belonging; they strive to excel in something, anything in what they consider will heighten a sense of self worth; they are masochists and feel at home in prisons. Therefore, they need treatment not punishment. (3)

Philosopher's email: How would a psychologist know these four characteristics of hardened criminals unless they were the results of many personal interviews? If so, they may then escape the charge that the psychologist's claims are nothing but interpretations of criminal minds.

Prison Warden: I hereby declare an end to the trialogue. You are all free to depart except Mr. Osama bin Laden whom we officials declare a "person of interest."

Discussion

1. Give two examples of the law of retaliation, which you saw in the news lately or elsewhere.

2. Do you believe this dictum: Let the punishment fit the crime? Explain.

3. Explain the retribution theory with one example.

4. Explain the utilitarian theory with one example.

5. Explain the revenge theory with two examples.

6. Critique the revenge theory.

7. Which of the three theories do you prefer and why?

8. Are the four psychological reasons (why good results do not apply to hardened criminals) facts or interpretations? Explain the difference.

9. If the superintendent of the state prison requested your advice on how to rehabilitate prisoners, what two suggestions would you offer?

10. Can you explain the annotation attached to Selected Bibliography, chap.17, number 1?

11. Why does this seem reasonable to you? Punish criminals for what they did, not for who they are.

12. Do you believe that there is a two-tiered system of justice in the United

States: one for the wealthy (who frequently "get off") when they commit a crime and one for the poor? Can you give an example from the news media?

13. Comment on the epigraph.

INTERLUDE

CHAPTER 18

What's A Happy Life? Can I Achieve It? The Happy Test

"Very little is needed to make a happy life."

Marcus Aurelius, Roman Emperor

Prologue by Miss Happy

A happy life is the pie in the sky, which every person strains to grab. Only a few clutch it. Some wriggle close by. Others fly halfway towards it, but most people hardly get off the ground to leap for it.

Whatever we do, we do it ultimately to reach happiness (Aristotle). Why do we go to school for an education? Prepare for a career? Make friends? Get married? Raise a family? We immerse ourselves in all these activities because we hope that they will speed us to a happy life.

Julia:	What's a happy life for religious people and can they achieve it?
Minister:	A happy life for the religious consists in doing God's will on earth by living a holy life and if they persevere, they will realize happiness if not on earth then certainly in heaven.
Anthony:	What's happiness on earth for the non-religious?
Miss Happy:	Happiness, a happy life, signifies to many non-religious and religious a high level of joyful excitement. It's unrealistic to expect to live on

such a high level all one's life. No one does, no one can. Some restless youths try it but soon become fatigued and disillusioned. We might settle for a workable definition of a happy life: a contented or interesting life with occasional highs of excitement.

Ida: Agreed! How do we reach out for this contented, interesting life?

Miss Happy: Four Western philosophers have wrestled vigorously with this baffling question. There are three B. C. Greeks: Aristotle, Epicurus, Zeno; the other, an Englishman, Bertrand Russell. I hired a medium to contact them for a séance.

Séance

Medium: Aristotle, are you there?

Aristotle: We have been listening to you on our other world Internet. We three Greeks down here have invited Russell for dinner so that all four can answer you. Here is my solution to what begets happiness: First, you must enjoy at least moderate health. "No man is happy on a rack." This axiom of mine has often been quoted on your planet. Second, you must earn a moderate income. No man is happy on a starvation diet. On the other side of the drachma ("coin" as you would say) you don't have to be a millionaire to be happy as many believe. Third, a moderate amount of pleasure will suffice, not over-indulgence. (What a shame to have read on the Internet last night that half of the

Americans are overweight.) Fourth, as to knowledge, you don't have to be as learned as I; but no one is happy if he's an ignoramus. By the way, a choice piece of wisdom I picked up from the Internet, "If you think education is expensive, try ignorance." Fifth, you'll never be happy as a gangster but only as an honest person. Sixth, strive to be and have a "good" friend.

Epicurus: I accept Aristotle's laundry list on what produces happiness. I would simply emphasize the importance of repose or peace of mind.

Zeno: My school of stoics subscribes to Aristotle's laundry list and to Epicurus' footnote. In addition, we stoics are distinguished by the two badges of duty and indifference. Regarding duty we were smiling a century ago when we caught the British aphorism on our short wave: " England expects every man to do his duty." We have always preached a threefold duty — a duty to the gods (you would say "God" or "religion"), to country, and to family. The other badge, indifference, means that we train ourselves to be indifferent to feelings in order to develop self-control (which is in short supply). For example, if a neighbor insults us we don't shoot him, we ignore his remark by not allowing it to pass our chest and into our heart to stir up anger. We remain calm and that's why your dictionary calls us "stoical." Some stoics exaggerate indifference by shutting out sad

	feelings even when a family member dies. My time is up. Here is Bertrand Russell who emigrated from your planet in 1970.
Russell:	I'll hum along in harmony with the three Greeks and update them with the following necessities for a happy life: affection of and for the family, a wholesome job, ability to relax, and zest for life. By zest I mean the greater variety of interests, the greater the chances of happiness.
Medium:	Due to an earthquake in California on planet earth we've been cut off here in Pluto's netherworld.

Exercises (Courtesy of Pluto)

1. Comment on the following statement by the pessimistic German philosopher, Schopenhauer: "There is no more mistaken path to happiness than worldliness, revelry, high life."

2. Part of Bertrand Russell's legacy is a slate of seven causes of unhappiness: competition, fatigue, boredom, envy, excessive excitement, persecution mania, fear of public opinion. Write a one-half page paragraph on each of the seven causes or a two-page essay on one of them.

3. Discuss: there is unanimous agreement among psychologists and philosophers that happiness will never be attained if it's the direct goal of one's life. Only if you make another person or a cause the direct goal of your happiness will you indirectly achieve yours.

4. Comment on: "It is better to be Socrates dissatisfied than a pig satisfied," (John Stuart Mill).

5. Comment on the epigraph.

Take The Happy Test*

1.	Do I enjoy average health?	Yes	No
2.	Do I receive, at least, an average income?	Yes	No
3.	Do I love someone special and is my love returned?	Yes	No
4.	Am I moderately content with my conditions in school or work?	Yes	No
5.	Do I have a variety of interests in people and things?	Yes	No
6.	Am I capable of enjoying my leisure time?	Yes	No
7.	Do I have at least one good friend outside the family?	Yes	No
8.	Do I try to live a life of integrity?	Yes	No
9.	Do I strive to realize a goal in life?	Yes	No
10.	Do I radiate a friendly disposition toward most people I meet?	Yes	No
11.	Do I enjoy peace of mind?	Yes	No

*This test is compiled from the four Western philosophers.

Correction Key

If you answered Yes to any four or less questions, you are unhappy.

If you answered Yes to five, six or seven questions, you are happy sometimes.

If you answered Yes to eight, nine, ten or eleven questions, you are a happy person.

CHAPTER 19

There Can Only Be Three Types Of Friends

"Without friends no one would want to live, though he possessed everything else."

Aristotle

Aristotle dedicated his book on ethics to his son Nicomachus. The colossal Greek thinker taught that we humans can experience only three types of friends: the pleasant, the useful, the good friend.

The Pleasant Friend

Aristotle, "The Master of those who know" (Dante), writes with a frank quill about young people. He claims they search for pleasant friends of any available stripe: handsome friends, snappy entertaining talkers, jokers, etc. As soon as the pleasure evaporates so does the friendship. That's why two or three pleasant friendships arise and fall even in a single day.

Sharing Period

Share vignettes with others about some pleasant friends you encountered in life, movies, literature, the Bible.

Reading Period

1. In Oscar Wilde's story, "The Picture of Dorian Gray," do you agree or

disagree that the painter, Basil Hallward, liked Dorian Gray simply because the latter was strikingly handsome? Quote from the text of the story to support your answer.

2. In "A Streetcar Named Desire," a drama by Tennessee Williams, do you agree or disagree that the husband (played by Marlin Brando in the film version) did not love his wife but wanted her exclusively for his own sexual gratification? Quote from the text of the play to support your answer.

The Useful Friend

Useful friends, according to our Greek master, are friends because they need something from each other. They may not necessarily find pleasure in each other's company. If Judy likes Samantha because Samantha can help her every time her computer gets a stomachache, and Samantha likes Judy because Judy drives her to school, they are useful friends. When Judy's computer stays healthy she has no need of Samantha and when Samantha gets a ride to school from her boyfriend, she has no need of Judy. In a useful friendship you may have as many friends as you have needs. As your needs increase your friends increase; as your needs decrease your friends decrease.

Sharing Period

1. In Aristotle's opinion complaints arise more from useful friends than from pleasant friends. Agree? Disagree?

2. Friendship of utility seems a natural for people at opposite ends of the

spectrum: between educated and non-educated; between rich and poor. Why?

3. Share stories with others about some useful friends you met in life, movies, literature.

Reading Period

1. Talk about some useful friendships you may have read in the Bible. For instance, in the first book of Samuel, chapters 18-23, was David's friendship for Jonathan based on utility? Indicate the biblical text to support your answer.

2. In the novel, Washington Square (or in the video, The Heiress) by Henry James, would you consider Morris a useful friend or a pleasant friend or both in his treatment of Catherine? Indicate the passages in the text to support your answer.

The Good Friend

Good friends exemplify the ideal friendship. Its foundation rests on the solid integrity of both characters. It's because they are good persons that they are useful and pleasant to each other. Their goodness is grounded in virtues, (good habits). One important virtue is that of mutual trust. Also important are respect, esteem, mutual services without being asked, the sharing of joys and sorrows. All this activity takes place in frequent enjoyable visits.

Such virtues leave no room for jealousy, envy, duplicity or slander. As a consequence, their friendship will last as long as their goodness lasts and goodness is permanent whereas pleasure and utility are temporary. Throughout all his rapture in describing a good friendship, Aristotle strikes a sad note when he injects that we are lucky if we have just one or two good friends. (It's also unfortunate that he always talks about friendship among men. We will forgive him in spite of his brilliance. He was a product of his macho age.)

Sharing Period

1. Aristotle quotes two notable Greeks with opposite views on why good friends are attracted to each other: one said, "they are alike," and the other, "they are different." Offer your opinion.

2. Aristotle insists that a good friendship will not last long if the two friends don't spend a lot of time in each other's company. Name some modern ways in which friends may spend time together which were unavailable in the pre-information age of the Greeks.

3. According to Aristotle, for two persons to be good friends they must be equals, of the same station in life. But the following are not equals: father and son; (we'll add mother and daughter); husband and wife; king and subject.

   a) Critique the Big Greek.

b) What do husbands and wives mean when they say affectionately, "She/he is not only my wife/husband but also my friend."

4. Share some examples of good friends in the Aristotelian sense, whom you have encountered in your personal life, movies, literature, the Bible.

Reading Period

1. For the best biblical example of the friendship between two women, read the Book of Ruth. Discuss it.

2. For an example of good friends in literature, read about the friendship between Ramona and Alessandro in Helen Hunt Jackson's novel, <u>Ramona</u>. Discuss it.

Discussion on All Three Types of Friends

1. When the USA and Canada remind themselves in times of dispute that they are friends, which type of friendship do they mean? Give a reason for your answer.

2. When children say that they are friends, which type of friendship do they mean? Give a reason for your answer.

3. In your opinion what type of friendship would exist between two murderers, thieves, kidnappers? Why?

4. Which types of friends would more probably live longer together: two pleasant friends, two useful friends or two good friends? Why?

CHAPTER 20

There Are Only Three Reasons Why People Laugh (1)

"If we may believe our logicians, man is distinguished from all creatures by the faculty of laughter." (2)

Joseph Addison

Emcee: Did you ever ask yourself why people laugh? Although there are three theories competing to solve this puzzle, not one of them alone can explain the answer completely. All three theories acting together can stage a more than spectacular performance. Allow me to introduce the three theories by name. They are in order of appearance Sir Superiority, Mr. Surprise, and Miss Relief. First may I present Sir Superiority.

Sir Superiority: We laugh because we feel superior to others afflicted with misfortunes, faults or vices. Don't you enjoy a sense of superiority when you witness a friend suddenly struck by a blueberry pie? When your little brother makes a grammatical error?

Emcee: I present to you Mr. Surprise.

Mr. Surprise: We laugh because something unexpectedly happens. Two things collide that catch us by surprise. Oscar Wilde, while serving time in an English prison, bellowed, "If this is the way the queen treats her convicts, she doesn't deserve to have any." The surprise is that the word convicts is used where you would expect the words children or servants as in the statement, "If this is the way a mother treats her children she doesn't deserve to have any." George Wallace, the late governor of Alabama, is reputed to have refuted the charge that his rehabilitation record of prisoners was woefully inadequate, "It wasn't my fault. They sent me poor material."

Emcee: May I present to you the last hurrah, Miss Relief.

Miss Relief: We laugh because we feel liberated from the restrictions or restraints which society imposes upon our natural impulses. Society or good manners teach us that it's impolite to tell sexy jokes, yet we laugh when we hear them. Likewise, polite society dictates, "Thou shall not be rude." That commandment rules out insults inflicted on others but we admit that they can be comical though unkind. Again, society restrains us from talking nonsense, but the performance of nonsensical actions and mumbling nonsensical words can be entertaining.

End Man: Now that we patiently heard the three laughable theorists, how about some jokes?

Laughing Exercises

1. Tell your favorite joke and ask others to classify it according to one of the three theories above.

2. What type of humor does your favorite comedian use? Your favorite comic strip?

3. Give two examples of each of the three theories of laughter.

4. Write a one-page essay on how your sense of humor changed since you were a child.

5. Include examples of jokes you once considered funny. You may include examples from TV shows, TV comedians, and comic strips.

6. Could you defend one of three theories above to explain all the jokes you heard today?

7. The English novelist George Eliot once said that what a person laughs at is a fair indication of that person's level of culture. Write a two-page essay defending or refuting, with examples, this assertion.

8. The North American Laughter Club (3) claims that no jokes are needed to laugh uncontrollably and it's helpful for one's health. In your opinion, is the North American Laughter Club using the word "joke" to mean a physical sensation or is it using it according to one of the three definitions above?

9. Read your favorite joke book again or borrow one from a comical friend. Classify (according to the three theories) only those jokes that rock you with laughter.

10. Comment on the epigraph.

ETHICS

CHAPTER 21

How Am I Expected To Know The Difference Between Right And Wrong?

A Religious Ethical Style, A Philosophical Ethical Style, An Ethics Test

"The direction of a person's future life will depend on the starting point of his/her education."

Plato

Scene: A meeting of parents, teachers, students in a high school hall, 2:00 P.M.

Topic: Ethics

Principal: If your classmate suggests, "Let's start a fire in the wooded area outside our gated community to clock the arrival of the fire trucks," would you agree to ignite the fire because:

    you don't want to be called chicken?

    you want to be accepted by your peers?

    you want to prove you're a sport?

    you think it will be fun?

Judge: After the fire, when you are towed before my court and your clothes are reeking with smoke, would you feel comfortable to plead not guilty by offering one or more of the four reasons above? I doubt it.

Alice: How about giving us some guidelines.

Four Ethical Guidelines

School philosopher: The most general guideline or ethical rule states: Do good and avoid evil. But "good" and "evil" are too general. A breakdown of "do good" into four time-honored, trusty, ethical guidelines would be more specific. One: Would my action harm others? My conscience will whisper to me what "harm" means; it will be correct most of the time. Like a beacon in the stormy sea of life, it will warn me from smashing against the cliffs of lying, stealing, etc. Two: Would I honestly, sincerely want others to do to me what I do to them? Would I want my action to become a universal law? For example, if I judge it's OK for me to bash someone's nose once a week for my weekly exercise, would I honestly, sincerely want others to do the same to my nose? Would I want my action to become a universal law? The universal, moral, justifiable law would state that anyone may bash someone's nose including my own, once a week for exercise. Three: What are the consequences of my action? No one can foresee all the consequences of an action, but we can all foresee some immediate consequences. Four: Does the end (the intention) justify the means (the measures adopted to carry out the intention)? Here is an ethically correct example of the end justifying the means: Joan's intention of buying a car is realized by the means of getting a job. However, if Joan stole money (evil means) to buy the car (good intention), the good intention would not justify the means (stealing).

Principal: Those four guidelines above will go a long way to set up an ethical tone in our school.

Get A Life: Get An Ethical Style

English Teacher: Just as I help students to develop a writing style, so should other teachers help students to develop an ethical style, a particular way of solving problems of right and wrong.

Katie: My minister and parents taught me a religious ethical style. It's simple and practical. Whenever I'm hesitating between a sinful and a right action, I ask myself "What would Jesus do?" I have no trouble in finding the correct answer. It works for me.

Tara: My guru and parents also taught me a religious ethical style. I automatically ask myself "What would Buddha do?" It works for me.

Chaplain: All religious people have a religious ethical style be they Jews, Muslims, etc.

Irene: What about us who were brought up properly but not in a particular religion? With what kind of ethical style can we live?

Philosopher: You can live with a philosophical ethical style. There are various types but I'll describe my own. It consists of three yardsticks. Whenever you are trying to decide between a right or wrong action, apply one or more of the three following yardsticks. In some cases, one yardstick will solve the doubt, but in others you may have to use two or all three. Try them. You'll like them. Practice makes perfect but first here are three hot preliminaries.

Three Hot Preliminaries

No philosophical ethical style will solve problems with 100% clarity.

The more facts you know about the problem the more ammunition you'll have to solve it.

In most complex problems you'll have to settle for the least erroneous answer. C'est La Vie!

Wendy: When are you going to give us the three yardsticks for a philosophical ethical style? I got a purse full of problems to solve.

Three Ethical Yardsticks (1)

Philosopher: First, ask yourself may I apply the principle of The Greatest Good for the Greatest Number?

Mr. Hardnails: We parents apply this ethical yardstick whenever we make house rules. For example, I ruled that all my four children must observe the eleven o'clock curfew and our 19-year-old daughter objected. She complained that eleven is too early to walk out of the dance hall and surrender boyfriends to competitors who remain till midnight. I fired back, "That's the rule, Anne." I suppose this would be an example of the Greatest Good for the Greatest Number. The greatest number would refer to my other three children.

State Senator: The ideal is to craft a law that would include as many people as possible. That's why we lawmakers often appeal to the greatest good for the greatest number principle. But any lawmaker in city hall, state legislature or congress will assure you that comprehensive laws are difficult to formulate.

Philosopher: The second yardstick of our adopted philosophical ethical style is to ask "Am I violating anyone's individual right(s)?" In applying the ethical standard of the greatest good for the greatest number, I must always ask whether that rule violates the right(s) of others. In Mr. Hardnails' example, his 19-year-old daughter would have to persuade her father that her right to dance till midnight is being violated. Good luck, Anne.

Mayor: An instance of violating the rights of others in the application of the greatest good for the greatest number would be a town council's decision that only the citizens who live north of the town hall may vote and the sprinkling of Asian Americans who live south of the town hall may not vote. This decision of the town council would be obviously unethical because it violates the rights of the few.

Councilman: The Mayor's example glaringly illustrates how a majority can easily tyrannize a minority even in a democratic country.

Chief-of-police: Nonetheless, there are occasions when personal rights may be suspended temporarily because of the greatest good for the greatest number. If the police, for example, ordered a neighborhood to remain indoors until they found the lurking murderer, this violation of restricting the neighbors' freedom would be justified.

Chorus: Hail to the Chief!

Philosopher: The third yardstick of our ethical style is to ask, may I apply the ethical yardstick of "B and B," — burdens vs. benefits? There are ethical situations when yardstick one — the greatest good, and yardstick two — individual rights, may not be as applicable as burdens vs. benefits. This B and B ethical rule applies to situations in which burdens vs. benefits must be balanced. If the burdens far exceed the benefits, it would be ethical to reject the burdens. If the employer imposes burdens on the employee for which burdens he refuses to pay an adequate salary, the employer acts unethically and the protesting employee acts ethically.

Mrs. Noble: Sometimes our children think that we parents impose burdens that exceed benefits.

English Teacher: I bet that I can teach a writing style faster than the school philosopher can teach an ethical style even though it has only three yardsticks — the greatest good for the greatest number, individual rights, and burdens vs. benefits.

Audience applauds as meeting ends.

Beginner's Conscience Training

From the four ethical guidelines select one or more to decide between a right and wrong action in the following situations. Explain your answer.

Sample: Philip needs money to help his father pay the rent. May he sell drugs? Answer: No because of ethical guideline #4. I explain. The end does not justify the means. The end is good, to help his father pay the rent, but the means, selling drugs are wrong.

1. Sam does not like African Americans. May he set fire to the home of the African American family at the edge of town where the fire won't spread too widely? Answer yes or no because of ethical guideline #___. Explain.

2. Celeste's employer at the supermarket draws a large salary but Celeste draws a small one. She needs money more than he does. May she dip her small hand in the till? Answer yes or no because of ethical guideline #___. Explain.

3. May Benjamin drive his Ford in a zigzag style to see if the local cop is on the job? Answer yes or no because of ethical guideline #___. Explain.

Advanced Conscience Training

Of the three ethical yardsticks (above) offered as a philosophical ethical style, select one or more to explain your choice in the following two cases.

1. David says to Carol, "We've seen so many movies on how to stab people to death. How about coming with me Saturday night to stab Mrs. Pound just to see how it feels in real life?" How should Carol decide?

2. After Harry wrecked two cars, he was itching to speed-test his new sports car (a birthday gift from his parents). He invited his girlfriend, Sally, and another couple, their best friends, for a Tuesday night race on the new highway with little or no traffic. The couple agreed excitedly. Should Sally accept the invitation?

Discussion

Stanley: The only way I know whether an action is right or wrong is to go ahead and do it. Afterwards, I'll find out whether I did the right or wrong thing so that I'll know what to do the next time around. Critique Stanley's principle of deciding between a right and wrong action.

Philosopher: During high school years various moral issues inevitably arise in connection with various curriculum subjects. An author (2) identified four typical value systems that teachers use to answer the students' moral questions. One: The teacher does not answer the students' moral question but changes the subject. Two: The teacher avoids the controversial question (e.g., have gays/lesbians rights?) and answers by presenting values and virtues that all can agree on (fairness, kindness). Three: The teacher stresses the importance of expressing one's own values rather than discuss whether some values are moral or not. Four: The teacher answers a controversial question by not taking sides but allowing all points of view, moral and immoral. The moral guidelines and yardsticks in this chapter are offered to answer moral questions. Would you agree or disagree that they are more helpful to answer moral questions than any of the four typical teachers' answers above?

An Ethics Test Drafted By Tenth Grade Students

1. Do you cheat in tests?
2. Do you destroy school property?
3. Do you lie?
4. Do you copy homework?
5. Do you cause injury?
6. Do you "graffiti" on walls?
7. Do you damage a person's reputation?
8. Do you disobey school rules?
9. Would you beat up a person for not helping to cheat?
10. Do you use drugs?
11. Do you drink alcohol?
12. Do you steal?
13. Do you respect those in authority?
14. Do you provoke violence?

15. Do you lie to protect yourself at the cost of others?
16. Do you steal from open lockers or unguarded property?
17. Do you kill plants?
18. Are you rude to the teachers?
19. Do you make fun of others?
20. Do you neglect homework?
21. Do you write on white boards with permanent pens?
22. Have you committed adultery?
23. Does violence stimulate you?
24. Would you go out of your way to inflict great pain on others?
25. Are you untrustworthy?
26. Are you unable to keep secrets?
27. Do you approve if you see abnormal behavior?

Exercises

1. Indicate which of the 27 questions concern the violation of personal individual rights, i.e., the second ethical yardstick explained above.
2. What would you add to this test? What would you eliminate and why?
3. In your opinion, rearrange the 27 questions in order of importance.
4. Comment on the epigraph.

CHAPTER 22

A Chart Of Lies: A Way Of Life? Or Be Myself?

"When in doubt tell the truth. You will confound your enemies and astound your friends."

Mark Twain

"Oh, what a tangled web we weave when first we practice to deceive."

Walter Scott

Data

1. There is no agreement on the strict definition of a lie.

2. There is no agreement on the kinds of lies, their number, their names, their justification.

3. Webster's Dictionary offers three definitions: "to make an untrue statement with intent to deceive," "to create a false or misleading impression," and "to convey an untruth."

4. The following is a more complete working definition: A lie is any intended deception communicated via spoken or written words, silence, signs, acts, (e.g., forgery). "Intended" signifies that the liar is fully aware that he does not believe in his own communication. (1)

Type of Lie	Example	Justifiable or Not?
White lies, fibs: said with no intent to injure or deceive	Flattery, boasting, social expressions ("I've a previous engagement")	Justifiable, generally
Lies to children and to the incapacitated	Coaxing a child out of a burning house	Justifiable. It's wrong to tell children lies just because they are children
Lies to liars	A pathological liar (or mythomaniac) known to all and harmless	Unjustifiable. To lie to such a liar may make him feel justified in lying
Lies to liars	A frequent liar	Unjustifiable. Lying to teach him a lesson is ineffective
Lies to criminals	A murderer asks if his "victim" is in your house	Justifiable to avoid harm
Lies to teachers	Cheating in exams, plagiarism, blaming parents for undone homework	Unjustifiable
Lies by advertisers and corporations	False qualities attributed to products: tobacco, cars, health pills, food	Unjustifiable

Type of Lie	Example	Justifiable or Not?
Medical lies to patients	Placebos	Justifiable, only after subjects consented
Lies to the sick and dying	Patients who dislike bad news, or who may be harmed by true information	Unjustifiable, except in rare cases, but even then someone close to the patient must receive correct information
"Loyal" lies to protect colleagues, especially doctors	An incompetent doctor	Unjustifiable. "Loyalty" is overruled by the moral obligation to prevent fatalities
Lies by doctors, lawyers, ministers to protect confidentiality of clients	Lies told by doctor to parents asking if daughter is pregnant	Justifiable, if parents accept that doctors are expected to lie about such questions
Lies by doctors, lawyers, ministers to protect confidentiality of clients	Priest lies to police about a penitent's admission of murder	Justifiable. Police have no moral right to ask priests questions re confessions
Lies by doctors, lawyers, ministers to protect confidentiality of clients	Lawyer lies to jury about the innocence of his client	Unjustifiable. Lawyer should refuse the case because his lies do not justify

Type of Lie	Example	Justifiable or Not?
Lies about scientific research	Advances in new products and methods to cure diseases	Unjustifiable. The motive is usually money and /or fame
Lies by the government to the public	President Johnson's undeclared war in Vietnam	Unjustifiable. Insufficient reason to lie to the citizenry

Discussion

1. Comment on the following saying: Awareness is the first stage of curing oneself of lying.

2. Offer and discuss one lie you recently heard on TV, radio or in conversations.

3. Do you agree with this statement? The amount of trust and esteem in a liar diminishes when the lies are found out. Explain.

4. Explain this statement with an example: if one habitually tells the truth, one will not readily lie when tempted.

5. Expand on this statement: We should avoid telling lies lest we contribute to the public notion that lying is acceptable in society.

6. Comment: Not to lie is to say no to a world that is overly saturated in a flood of lies in the social, business, and political arenas, e. g., the CEOs of

Enron and World Com.

7. Comment on the two epigraphs.

An Infernal Contest

Dante's Divine Comedy condemns Ulysses for his numerous lies, and sits him in the Eighth Circle of Hell. Draw nine circles of hell and place the following in the circles you think they deserve. Begin with the first circle (the smallest in the center of the page) for the worst liars and work outwards.

You may prefer to nominate your own nine candidates in lieu of the suggested nine listed here, in no particular order of importance: advertisers, lawyers, used car dealers, politicians, government officials, salesmen, athletic drug users, business people, CEOs.

MID-TERM SELF-EXAMINATION

CHAPTER 23

In Which Of The Six States Of Moral Development Am I?

"Virtue is harder to acquire than knowledge and, if lost in a young man, is seldom recovered."

John Locke

As we grow physically so does our notion of right vs. wrong grow morally.

Child

Stage 1 — Children learn what's right and wrong from outside of themselves especially from parents. Children gaze upon situations exclusively from their own point of view and have no ability to consider the viewpoint of others.

Stage 2 — Children gradually become aware that others possess similar needs and desires. They try to manipulate others to get what they themselves want. Their criterion for right vs. wrong is self-interest.

Youth

Stage 3 — The criteria for right vs. wrong are conformity and loyalty to the actions and attitudes of parents, brothers, sisters, teachers, classmates, friends.

Stage 4 — The criteria for right vs. wrong are conformity and loyalty to one's own nation through the obedience of laws. Youths now see that they and others form part of a larger social system. They begin to subordinate individual needs to those of the group.

Adult

Stage 5 — Criteria for right vs. wrong are reached by compromise, agreement, contracts, due process. Why? Because adults are aware of all different values in society. Values of others must be accepted or at least tolerated.

Stage 6 — Criteria for right vs. wrong are reached by universal principles, e.g., the greatest good for the greatest number, the avoidance of violating individuals' rights, the evaluation of burdens vs. benefits as explained in chap. 21. (1)

Note: The purpose of the six-stage schema above is not accuracy. It is intended to challenge ourselves to locate which stage we graduated from, in what stage we are presently living, and into which stage we would like to move.

Working out with the Six Stages

Give one reason for your opinion on the following:

1. If your cousin proclaimed to you, "I'm a Republican (Democrat) because mother and her friends have belonged to the Republican (Democratic) Party for generations," in which of the six stages would you place her?

2. A young man once shouted to his professor of ethics, "I don't want to decide what's right and wrong; just tell me what I'm supposed to do." In which stage is he living? To which stage does he want the professor to lead him? To which stage should the professor encourage him?

3. When you hear a tough American sloganize: "My country right or wrong," what stage is he definitely not inhabiting?

4. If friends confess to you, "We don't know the reasons for or against abortion. We're against it because our church is against it," in which stage are they living?

5. In which stage do you think most of your friends live?

6. In which stage do you think most Americans live?

7. In which stage is it the most difficult to live?

8. Why is it difficult to inhabit stage six?

9. Do you know anyone who lives in stage six?

10. Comment on: "It's easier to construct a child than to repair an adult." (anonymous)

11. Comment on the epigraph.

ETHICAL ISSUES

CHAPTER 24

Gambling: Crime? Entertainment?

"I am a lost man . . . the great thing is will power." (1)

Dostoyevsky

A Digest of The Gambler by Fyodor Dostoyevsky

Alexey Ivanovitch is a tutor in the family of a Russian general. They tour German spas where gambling is the preferred sport. Astley, an English moneylender, and Alexey are rivals for the hand of Polina, the general's stepdaughter. Polina savagely amuses herself by repeatedly rejecting Alexey's heart-breaking expressions of love.

The elderly general fires off frequent telegraphs to his aunt in Moscow. He is impatient for news of her death so that he can inherit her fortune. The aunt, not as ill as the general had hoped, boards a fast train to Paris and bursts unannounced into his lavish hotel suite. She scolds him for squandering his wealth.

With Alexey as her casino coach, the aunt is excitedly initiated into the mysteries of roulette. As her winnings pile up in front of her bulging spectacles, her aged frame shakes with joy. By sunset, however, she loses heavily.

The crack of dawn finds her back at the casino. She thirsts for revenge. Her feverish brain guarantees that this time she will win. After a day of thrilling ups followed by discouraging downs, again, the sun sets on her losses.

At daybreak the aunt borrowed money from Astley to return to Moscow. Her gambling debts were such that her extensive estates had dwindled to a few scattered buildings.

When rumor reaches Alexey's ears that Polina needs rubles, he dashes to the roulette wheels, wins a fortune in a day's work, and casts it at her feet. With a sarcastic laugh she flings it into his face. She prefers to borrow money from Astley. A crestfallen Alexey soothes his pain by splurging his winnings on Mlle. Blanche.

Soon afterwards, Alexey, now a veteran gambler, returns to the familiar casino tables of the fashionable German spas. One day, lady luck abandons him so rudely that he wakes up in the debtor's prison.

Meanwhile the general married the youthful Mlle. Blanche. Within a month he died of a stroke in a Parisian restaurant and left her the diminished inheritance received from his deceased Moscow aunt.

On a somber day in Hamburg, Germany, Alexey chances upon Astley. The latter informs him that Polina really loves Alexey and desires his return. She is ill in Switzerland, in the care of Astley's family. Ecstatic Alexey agrees to return. But he is overwhelmed by a wave of doubts. Is he, a lifelong gambler, capable of reform? Has he the moral fiber to begin an honorable life to gain Polina's respect?

My interpretation of Dostoyevsky's deliberate obscure ending is that Polina had always rejected Alexey because he was a gambler with no purpose in life. In despair, Alexey concludes that the final cure awaits him in the grave.

Scene: Gamblers' roundtable in a back room of a Las Vegas hotel

Gambler No. 1: Since we are of such top-flight importance to be labeled "Knights of the green table" we may well ask, how do psychologists describe us?

Gambler No. 2: They paint us with the same colorful description that Dostoyevsky paints himself as the gambler in the novel of that name. In real life he finally conquers his vice. I think that the psychological portrait of a gambler is as follows. The gambler constantly sniffs for dangerous excitement available only at the tables of the "temples of chance." He knows in his head that the laws of probability weigh against him. He feels in his heart that certainly this time lady luck will be by his side. As he sweeps up his winnings he resembles a drunkard and cannot stop even when he loses. A professional gambler will bet his last meal ticket — as the gambler does in the novel — and choose to starve if he must.

Gambler No. 3: Dostoyevsky depicts the gambler and himself during his gambling career, as worthless and despised by friends and foes. Yet, the gambler in the novel had no obligation to anyone: not to a wife, family, friends. Whenever he lost money, down to the last kopeck, he would pick up a job as tutor or borrow rubles and play again at his adopted tables. There is nothing immoral about his lifestyle, though far from admirable. I wager that he was a "moral gambler" even if it sounds like an oxymoron. Do I have any takers?

Gambler No. 4: I object. If the Dostoyevskian gambler were an American gambler in our present society, corroding his life and disintegrating his personality like that, we would ask, "What happens when he gets ill?" He would be rushed to emergency at taxpayers' expense. What if he were called to military duty to defend his country in time of war? He would be declared physically unfit due to such a decayed lifestyle. We would then stamp his life as immoral.

Gambler No. 5: Moreover, a veteran gambler is a caricature of a citizen who contributes nothing to his country whose benefits he shamelessly enjoys. Now my question: Why do many non-gamblers point the finger at us when they themselves indulge in countless styles of gambling?

Gambler No. 6: Name three.

Gambler No. 5: Insurance, stocks, bonds.

Gambler No. 6: Name four more.

Gambler No. 5: Lotteries, slot machines — in casinos and on ships, horse and dog racing. Want more?

Gambler No. 6: Yes.

Gambler No. 5: Bingo, pools, raffles.

Gambler No. 6: Stop. Enough. Will someone grab Webster's Dictionary and flip to the definition of gambling to see whether it agrees with the ten gambling types you so eloquently listed. (2)

Gambler No. 1: Bingo. All ten agree. "The act or practice . . . of playing a game and consciously risking money or other stakes in its outcome . . . an uncertain event."

Gambler No. 5: Let's go on the offensive and ask again. Is gambling moral?

Gambler No. 6: In the last 50 years America has rolled out the welcome mat for legalized gambling.

Gambler No. 1: Withdraw that statement from the table. It's not answering the question.

Gambler No. 2: I'll gamble this opinion. Gamblers play morally whenever they lose no more money than they can afford to lose. In place of a usual amount of money set aside for entertainment, they gamble it on the "green."

Gambler No. 3: In other words, a person may gamble morally if the amount of cash gambled remains relative to the size of his wallet. A company manager may throw away more gambling money than his employee.

Gambler No. 4: For example, a bread winner of a family gambles immorally if he/she gambles away money to such an amount that the family would be deprived of a sufficiency for food, bills, and household necessities.

Gambler No. 5: Besides the moral question there are others. Is gambling an uncontrollable illness? (3) I'm a member of Gamblers Anonymous. I should not even be spotted in your company.

Gambler No. 6: I differ from the view of your organization that compulsive or uncontrollable gambling is a disease. First, there is no scientific proof of such an illness. Second, to call compulsive gambling a disease encourages gamblers like ourselves to feel self-pity, to feel relieved of responsibility. Third, therapists might profit from classifying compulsive gambling as an illness.

Gambler No. 5: Believe what you want. I'm agitated about being a member of Gamblers Anonymous and nobody has ever asked how I would advise young people. I'll offer my advice anyway. Thou shall not begin to gamble. Thou shall not lend an ear to advertisers who make gambling attractive or fun. Thou shall not toy with the fancy of stopping your education, picking up a fortune in Las Vegas, retiring in the lap of greenbacks. Even if that fantasy materialized, you would never have developed your self- esteem in a normal, human manner of living.

Gambler No. 2: Let's turn the roulette wheel for another question. Does casino and Mississippi riverboat gambling enrich the local and state economies? I'll gamble in favor of a yes answer. Such gambling enriches through tax revenues, tourism, sales, businesses, construction jobs,

	infrastructure improvements of roads and bridges. Benefits are evident in the increase of property values and in money for schools.
Gambler No. 3:	I roll the dice differently. Gambling does not enrich local and state economies. The tax revenues are swallowed up in government costs to criminal courts and to prisons. Gambling attracts criminals. Gambling regulations cost money. Riverboat casinos haul away businesses from competitors and ruin local economies.
Gambler No. 4:	I don't believe that it's a question of either/or. I believe that some places profit overall, e.g., Las Vegas and other cities in Nevada. On the other side of the dice, there are gambling cities that do not profit.
Gambler No. 5:	An interesting question is that of the Native American casinos. I'll wager that gambling helps Native Americans. They receive more money for education, health, jobs, and more tribes own their own businesses.
Gambler No. 6:	I'll roll my dice against that view. Native American gambling does not help them. Revenues are not high and their casinos attract crime and maybe organized crime.
Gambler No. 1:	I conclude this argument by saying that some Native Americans succeed, for instance Foxwoods in Connecticut (4) and some fail.
Gambler No. 2:	My minor in college was religious studies. What does the Bible say about gambling?

Gambler No. 3: My major in college was biblical studies. There is no biblical text directly dealing with gambling. Some appeal to Exodus 20: 15, "Thou shall not steal." Whoever uses this text makes the assumption that the writer of these words is saying that gambling is stealing. The text itself in the original Hebrew is talking about stealing in general and not about gambling in particular.

Gambler No. 4: It's midnight. I hereby pronounce the closing of the two-hundredth meeting of our roundtable.

Gambling Exercises

1. After reading the digest of <u>The Gambler</u> and eavesdropping on the gamblers' roundtable, do you think that there are special types of people who are attracted to gambling? Explain.

2. What is your opinion about the argument between gamblers 3 and 4: can a person live the life of a moral gambler? Defend your answer with one or two reasons.

3. Gambler 5 rolls out ten examples of gambling. Do you think that one or two might arguably be opportunities for donations rather than examples of gambling? If so, which two?

4. Do you agree that gambling is moral when the money gambled is money set aside for entertainment as explained by gamblers 2 and 3? Explain why.

5. Give two examples of immoral gambling, i.e., gambling beyond one's means.

6. In your opinion is gambling an illness? Explain.

7. Do casino and riverboat gambling help local and state economies? Explain

your opinion.

8. Do you think that Native American gambling benefits their tribes? Explain.

9. If you methodically studied the age of car race-drivers, their records of wins and losses, the weight of the cars, the special features of the race tracks, you will not always win your bets for the simple reason that you will never know which races are "fixed." Name at least two other gambling sports where a similar methodical study will also fail.

10. Comment on the following: "Gambling houses and race tracts . . . depend not on probability for their income, but on a percentage of business done." (5)

11. Comment on the scandal of William Bennett who publicly moralized about virtues orally and in his book, The Book of Virtues. Later he was exposed as an addicted gambler.

CHAPTER 25

What's Pornography? What's Beauty?

"Education . . . has produced a vast population able to read but unable to distinguish what is worth reading."

Macaulay

A Town Meeting

Mayor: Last Monday the PTA stormed into my office and demanded to sweep pornography out of town.

English teacher: Before we chase away the plague let's ask Mr. Webster to define the three words relative to our powwow: pornography, erotica, obscenity. First, pornography: "A description of prostitutes." This is the meaning of the two Greek words, which gave birth to our English "pornography." Webster's other meaning: "A depiction (as in writing and painting) of licentiousness or lewdness." Allow me to amplify. Nowadays pornography is not only thought of "in writing or painting" but in sculpture, drama, dance, movies, TV, talk shows, books, magazines, newspapers, comic strips. Anything I forgot?

Mrs. Conservative: Permit me to inject that pornography paints sex as if it has no tie-in with procreation, true love, and commitment.

Mr. Flipback: Did my eardrums hear the teacher mention movies and TV? Don't we already have a classification of movies to guide parents? Can't parents control TV with a flip of the remote control? I agree however that busy parents have other fish to fry.

Mr. Allknow: We are on the prowl for a wider solution than classifications.

English teacher: Webster's third definition of pornography: "A portrayal of erotic behavior designed to cause sexual excitement." Erotic is defined as literary or artistic. Obscenity is defined as "filthy, disgusting to the senses . . . grossly repugnant . . ." I'll now accept an applause for the completion of my dictionary report.

Lawyer: Regarding the three definitions, please join me in the comforting words of Supreme Court Justice Potter Stewart. He admitted that he could not define pornography but knew it when he saw it. May I add that some people use all three words as synonyms for pornography. Obscenities often means fowl language.

Police Chief: What does the law say about pornography?

Judge: The federal law is ineffective because it's restricted by the first amendment's moral right of freedom of speech.

Mrs. Stone: What's free speech got to do with pornography?

Law student: The free speech amendment means that we are allowed to express our opinions. Some legalists defend the interpretation of the amendment to mean that pornography expresses an opinion, as "I hate women" and therefore pornography is protected by freedom of speech. Other legalists deny that pornography expresses an opinion.

Recording secretary: So far, we learned that in spite of Webster we don't know what pornography means and that the federal government does not know how to censor it.

Social Science teacher: Why demand censorship when it's so difficult to find definitive proof that pornography harms young people and adults?

Feminist (male): Do social scientists, psychologists, and government officials need elaborate surveys to prove that pornography degrades women? Many adults suffer no harm from pornography. But what about children? They have not yet attained maturity of judgment. They are easily persuaded by what they see especially when juicy pornography is flashed to them as permissible. Do you truly need proof that children are being harmed? Is it not a basic law that we learn by imitation? If children learn so many good things by imitation don't they also learn bad things by imitation? (Rumbling murmurs of approval)

Feminist (female): A report on the split in the feminist movement just in. Some feminists favor censorship of pornography because it projects women as pleasurable sex objects. Other feminists disfavor censorship because they fear their past, difficult but successful battles against censorship might reverse their gains.

Mr. Offtick: So if the government can't throw a roadblock against publishers and booksellers by means of censorship, how are we parents supposed to pull our children away from buying filth at the local bookstores?

Bookseller: What am I expected to answer sharp teenagers when they quote the first amendment?

Counselor: Why should intelligent citizens in a democracy wait for laws from Washington or the state capital?

Town manager: That's the solution. Why wait? Let each town in America organize itself beginning with ours. All we need is a long drink of goodwill to protect our youths. The adults can take care of themselves with their conscience as guide. We'll line up all the influential key players: the police chief, the judge, business leaders, professionals, religious leaders, teachers, PTA, other town societies. Together we can persuade booksellers, TV managers, theater owners to wash away the plague of pornography.

Mayor: All in favor say Aye.

Audience: Aye!

High school student: While I wait for the town to organize, what guideline can you give me about pornography?

Uninvited philosopher: Each individual may define pornography as that type of writing or viewing that stirs him/her to imagine and suggest acts contrary to conscience. Now that's a tailor-made definition of pornography.

Mayor: Meeting adjourned till next week. We will return with organizational plans that will serve as the model for every town in the nation.

Discussion

1. How would you grade the performance of the town meeting? Circle one and offer a reason for your grade: excellent, very good, good, failure.
2. With which speaker would you agree the most? Why? The least? Why?
3. State a reason why you would agree or disagree with the guideline offered by the uninvited philosopher.
4. State a reason why you would agree or disagree with many feminists who interpret the message of pornography to mean "I hate women."
5. If you accept the rough definition of pornography as filthy and erotica as artistic, what have you seen or read in the last month that qualifies as pornographic or erotica? Name it and say why it's filthy or artistic.
6. Suggest a movie, a play, a short story, a novel, a poem which in your opinion is pornographic or erotica and why.
7. Comment on the epigraph.

A Project in Six Steps

Step 1 Each student presents a plan to the class how he/she would organize the influential townspeople (listed by the town manager above) to flush out pornography.

Step 2   Because different students will offer some of the same ideas, elect a secretary who will record all the different ideas only once to avoid repetition.

Step 3   Elect a committee of three to write one organizational plan from all the ideas recorded by the secretary.

Step 4   One committee member will present the final plan to the class for an oral critique.

Step 5   Elect another secretary to write the final plan improved by the oral critique.

Step 6   Publish it in the school paper or local newspaper or both.

Optional project:

Adapt the steps of the above project to other town plagues: drugs, hate crimes, youth violence, etc.

What's Beauty?

"Love built on beauty, soon as beauty, dies."

John Donne

If you ever want to ignite a sizzling dispute, ask your friends, "What is beauty?" High schoolers may answer triumphantly, "Beauty is in the eye of the beholder." To which you might want to respond, "That definition refers to only one sense — the sense of sight. Give me a broader definition." To which a college friend might answer, "Beauty is whatever pleases the senses." To which you may learnedly reply, "That definition is so sweeping that it can accommodate everything from hot dogs to grand opera."

The traditional definition of beauty from the days of the ancient Greeks is unity in variety. A person, place or thing must be harmonious, decked out with balanced parts. (1) This definition reigned supreme, until it was yanked off its throne by our own contemporaries. They twist everything to fit the Greek definition, unity in variety, from a football pass to a splash of paint on a wall and to screeching blasts of dissonant symphonic music. Some aggressive contemporaries might even prefer the definition of beauty not as unity in variety but as disunity in variety. Herein lies the stalemate: because beauty is subjective, there is no winner in the contest for a definition of beauty. (2)

Beautiful Exercises

1. Which of the following three definitions of beauty do you prefer? If none, offer your own definition of beauty. Explain your preference, with at least one example, in a paragraph of six sentences or more. Beauty is in the eye of the beholder. Beauty is whatever pleases the senses. Beauty is unity in variety.

2. Should art produce morality? The three standard answers are: first, yes, because it's the traditional task of art to illustrate moral and religious truths as

in Christian and Buddhist art; second, yes, art should teach the values of the State as in Plato's Republic and in Marxism of the former Soviet Republic; third, no, enjoy art whether it's moral or immoral according to the slogan, "Art for art's sake." Defend your opinion.

3. Comment on the epigraph.

CHAPTER 26

Is Adolescent Sex Moral?

"Nature intends what man does not."

Thomas Aquinas?

An Intimate Conversation between Jill and Tom

Tom: I know that we are only 17 but look at all our friends who have been doing it since they were 15 and younger.

Jill: Is that your standard of morality? If all the people you know do something, then it's OK? By the way, let's use some of the debate rules we learned.

Tom: I see that you are serious. Let's clarify exactly what we want and don't want to talk about. (The first rule in a logical debate. Remember?) We will exclude petting, masturbation, and the controversy of sex education at home or at school. We'll focus on the real joy.

Jill: So we begin with you saying it's moral and I that it's immoral. Furthermore, we agreed about what we will debate but we have not decided how. Shall we allow arguments from religion?

Tom: Let's agree that religious people are against adolescent sex and admit that they are correct. We just want to debate this problem with non-religious arguments.

Jill: I admire the T-shirts worn by Louisiana students. "Abstinent I will stay until my wedding day. (1) Enough said. My position is that adolescent sex is immoral. I base my argument on the moral principle of benefits vs. burdens. I'll explain. For me as a girl the burdens far outweigh the benefits. Suppose something goes wrong and I become pregnant? The evil consequences are more disastrous for a girl than for a boy. Need I list them for you? First, where will I get the money for an abortion if I so choose? Second, if I choose to have the child, what happens to my remaining years at high school and college? I would have the burden of taking care of a child while continuing my education. Third, would not my choice of a career and a husband be automatically limited? Fourth, if you acted the coward and ran away from your paternal obligations, would that not pile another burden on my shoulders? Fifth, even if you decided out of duty to share my burdens, would it be a sincere marriage?

Tom: I refute all five evil consequences by answering that if we are both careful you will not get pregnant. Furthermore, you know as well as I do that a lot of our friends never had the problem of an unwanted pregnancy.

Jill: Your refutation is invalid because by your own insinuation you allow the probability that I may become pregnant no matter how many precautions we take. What about the few cases where there was an unwanted pregnancy?

Tom: It's time for me to offer an argument to support my position that it is moral to engage in adolescent sex. Nowadays 70% of 18 year olds have had intercourse. (2)

Jill: There you go again. You are appealing to numbers for morality. You are using a standard of morality according to what the crowd does. I already refuted you about this standard in my first statement when we began this discussion.

Tom: Aren't you a little old-fashioned? What's your idea of fun anyway? Ping-Pong?

Jill: If those rhetorical questions are meant as statements, and they are, I answer by reminding you that they are fallacies of "ad hominem," statements that attack my person rather than answer my objections.

Tom: The rumor mill of the guys is certainly true. I didn't expect you to be that tough.

Jill: Meaning what?

Tom: Never mind. I have an argument from authority. It's this. Many parents don't mind if their children wait till they are 18 or after high school graduation. Maybe it's because they are out of the house by then. (3) May I get back to you after graduation?

Jill: That's not an argument from authority. If the parents recommended adolescent sex at 18 from the depth of their wisdom rather than from the depth of their expediency then it could be accepted as an argument from authority and a poor one at that.

Tom: See you after graduation. (Waving good-bye)

Jill: (Waving and muttering) Typical male. He wants sex. I want love.

Discussion

1. In your opinion is there any moral difference between adolescent sex and premarital sex?

2. Add one or more to Jill's list of five evil consequences from pregnancy.

3. In Jill's philosophical ethical style she used the moral principle of benefits vs. burdens and not the greatest good for the greatest number principle nor did she use the individual rights principle. Of the three ethical principles (see chap. 21) do you approve or disapprove of her choice?

4. Which position do you accept, Jill's or Tom's and why? If neither explain yours.

5. Would a student who adopts a religious ethical style of total abstinence find anything objectionable in Jill's arguments? In Tom's arguments?

6. Do you find yourself (like Tom) solving personal moral problems by what

the majority of your peers think and do? Why does Jill think that it's an inadequate if not an immoral principle?

7. Should you or your parents be the first to raise the question of adolescent sex? Explain.

8. If you do not feel comfortable to speak with anyone in your immediate family about such personal questions, whom would you select outside your immediate family?

9. Give the pros and cons of sex education in the schools.

10. Do you see any connection between petting and the epigraph?

11. Discuss the questions that in your opinion should have been included in the ten questions above.

CHAPTER 27

The Rights Of Gays/Lesbians

"I know not whether laws be right, or whether laws be wrong."

Oscar Wilde

Gay Parade

Cast of characters: Sidewalk spectators

Chauffeur: Officer, why is Birch Street cordoned off?

Officer: It's the annual Gay parade celebration.

Clerk: It's a shame that there is so much misinformation stewing at the height of the information age.

Student: Name one.

Clerk: Many people falsely believe that homosexuals are pedophiles.

Carpenter: Name another misinformation.

Clerk: Homosexuality is contagious like a disease.

Teacher: Let's back up for definitions. Are gays and lesbians defined as homosexuals?

Bookworm: Yes. Webster defines homosexuality as "sexuality characterized by manifestation of sexual desire toward a member of one's own sex."

Purist: I heard the teacher say "gay." How sad it is that the beautiful word

	"gay" now means something different.
Skinhead:	They ruined an English word and society.
Mechanic:	How?
Skinhead:	They want as many rights as the heterosexuals.
Law student:	They are citizens and deserve the same rights as heterosexuals.
Bank teller:	What rights are they clamoring for?
Company manager:	They want domestic-partner benefits package from company employers just like heterosexuals get.
Employee:	That's only fair — equal pay for equal work.
Manager:	But the companies would be encouraging immoral living.
Employee:	A company has no legal or moral right to turn its flashlight on the bedroom of its employees. It's the company's obligation to give equal pay for equal work. That's a simple formula of justice.
Cab driver:	Name another right they are screeching for.
Custom officer:	They are yelling for the asylum rights of homosexual foreigners. Other Western nations grant them asylum.
Policeman:	America grants asylum to foreigners provided they can prove that the persecution chamber awaits them if we march them back to the motherland.
Cobbler:	What other rights do they scream about?
Soldier:	Military service.

Lieutenant:	The policy of don't ask, don't tell is working more or less. Let's leave it alone. Besides, homosexuals in the service have proven their worth just as the ancient Greek homosexual soldiers did.
Salesman:	Any other rights?
Counselor:	Yes. This is a big one. Why do gays and lesbians fight for the right to marry?
Judge:	Because marriage gives several economic and social benefits. For example, only spouses and immediate family are allowed in the emergency room.
Therapist:	Children raised by homosexuals will be at risk. School children will ridicule them. Many social situations will surface where both parents and children will be embarrassed and insulted.
Nurse:	Those risks can be overcome. You need stronger arguments. For instance, if you could prove that children of same sex parents will grow up as perverts, you would have a solid argument. There is no such proof and I doubt if one will ever appear on the medical psychological landscape. On the contrary, even before gays broke out of the closet, well-adjusted boys were reared by their aunts with no man involved.
Minister:	But what will happen to tradition? The traditional marriage has always been between man and woman.

Philosophy student: Socrates taught that a society must reexamine its traditions periodically. It's time to examine whether the marriage tradition of male and female may allow a change.

Teacher: So far, we have been chatting about homosexuals from the legal viewpoint. What about the moral viewpoint?

Social worker: Before we hike up to the moral plateau I assume we all agree that gay/lesbian love can be just as genuine in terms of commitment and mutual caring as heterosexual love.

Caregiver: Yes. We need not surf the Internet for reliable statistical studies on caring. Observed examples and anecdotal evidence suffice.

Philosopher: Since the teacher raised the moral aspect, please allow me to ask, "Is same gender sex immoral? In my unpopular and unsolicited opinion, same gender sex is immoral only if you accept nature as a criterion. Mother Nature's law obviously dictates that the construction of human bodies is such that a male body is fashioned to copulate exclusively with a female body. Therefore, the copulation of same sex bodies is unnatural and immoral. (This argument is more forceful against males than females.)

Bible student: So far you all spoke, prudently, legally, morally. What about biblically? There are biblical texts that condemn homosexuality especially St. Paul in 1 Corinthians 6:9, "neither the immoral nor

	idolaters, nor adulterers nor sexual perverts . . . will inherit the kingdom of God." (1) No matter how differently biblical scholars translate the two Greek words (malakoi, aresnokotai) they refer to homosexuals. Paul is even clearer in Romans 1:27. (2)
Biblical scholar:	I agree. But Paul condemns homosexual lust not homosexual love. Jesus does not mention homosexuality.
Policeman:	While you were all gossiping, the parade passed you by. You can catch up with it if you cut through that alley.

Gay Discussion

1. Do you feel that you can discuss the homosexual problem with your emotions under control?

2. Do you believe that homosexuality is not a choice? That it is determined before birth?

3. Do you agree with the employee who objects to companies asking about the life styles of employees? Explain.

4. Should America grant asylum to foreign homosexuals? Explain.

5. What's your opinion about the military policy of don't ask, don't tell?

6. Expand on your view of whether homosexuals should be granted the legal status of marriage.

7. What do you think of the minister's argument defending tradition?

8. Critique the philosopher's argument about same sex immorality.

9. With what type of arguments do you feel more comfortable: arguments based on the law, prudence (practicality), morality, the Bible? Explain why.

10. Name a movie or video, which you consider unfair to gays/lesbians. Why?

11. Name a movie or video, which you consider fair to gays/lesbians. Why?

12. Comment on the epigraph.

CHAPTER 28

What's All This Shouting About Abortion?

"Men never do evil so completely and cheerfully as when they do it from religious conviction."

Pascal

A One Act Play

Place: Across the street from an abortion clinic.

Time: A hot afternoon at 3 P. M.

Actors: Two groups of 12 confronting each other with placards. Many passersby.

Unemployed teacher:	Because the abortion issue is so overly charged with emotion, I consulted Webster's Dictionary and streamlined his definition of abortion to suit the occasion.
Both groups:	Let's hear it.
Teacher:	Abortion is a deliberate expulsion of a woman's fetus any time before completion of pregnancy.
Doctor:	I'll diagram some medical facts in my clinic and hang them on a placard from this window as a background for an intelligent debate.

INTERCOURSE AND CONCEPTION

⇒SPERM MEETS EGG: One cell contains 46 pairs of chromosomes.
 ⇒IN 13 DAYS: 16 cells appear.
  ⇒IN 2 WEEKS A ZYGOTE is implanted in the uterus wall.
   ⇒IN 2 MONTHS AN EMBRYO: Organ system and brain waves develop.
    ⇒AFTER 2 MONTHS a fetus develops.
     ⇒IN 5-7 MONTHS, VIABILITY: The fetus can survive outside the womb.

Drive-by lawyer: Remember that abortion is legal up to three months of pregnancy according to the 1973 U.S. Supreme Court decision Roe vs. Wade.

Town clerk: Thank you, Mr. Lawyer. We are not talking about the legal but the moral issue. Is it moral or immoral for a woman to abort? Does everyone agree `that what makes abortion immoral is the killing of a human life?

Philosopher: So the precise issue of the abortion debate should be, "When does human life begin?"

Opera singer: Oh, doctor. Oh Doctor. When, Oh when does human life begin?

Doctor: I cannot answer that question. (He shuts the window.)

Scientist: I overheard that. The doctor is on target. We scientists stick to empirical facts — facts proven by the senses. We can tabulate the increase of a fetus' brain waves and, if at a certain frequency you decide it's a human being, be my guest. Also, we can trace the development of the fetus' organs and, if at a certain stage you decide

	it's a human being, be my guest.
Pastor:	As an anti-abortionist, enlightened by how lawyers and scientists think, may I add how religious people think?
Anti-abortionists:	Aye! Aye! You tell them Reverend!
Pastor:	Both pro-abortionists and anti-abortionists agree that at conception there is no actual human life, but there is potential human life. In other words, everybody knows that the end product will not crawl out in nine months as a jackrabbit, but as a human being.
Philosopher:	Congratulations, Pastor. You spoke with the razor-edge precision of a philosopher when you differentiated between a potential from an actual human being. That distinction spells the exact division between the pro and the anti-abortionists. The pro-abortionists insist that abortion is at least morally allowed until the fetus develops to the stage of actual human life.
Nurse:	Nobody knows at what precise period of time the fetus becomes human.
Philosopher:	The closer the fetus develops into a human being, the more difficult it becomes to justify abortion.
Lawyer:	That's correct and that's why the law says that three months is a reasonable point in time, after which abortion is illegal.
Pregnant woman:	I don't mean to spoil the party, but since you are all gathered here,

armed with your rights to discuss people like myself, not one of you ever asked me whether I have any rights.

Anti-abortionist: Rights? What rights?

Philosopher: She's right. Pregnant women have a right of privacy. Because the fetus is a part of her body, she may morally appeal to the right of privacy.

Bank clerk: The philosopher is right. If citizens appeal to their right of privacy when they are violated by the stealth of their credit card numbers, what could be more private than a part of your own body?

Reverend: She has no rights because of a higher law of God (waving his Bible in the air) who forbids all abortions after conception.

Atheist: Many biblical scholars say that you cannot prove that the Bible forbids abortion. Even if the Bible did forbid abortion, you would be entitled to your religious belief, but you have no right to impose it on other Americans who are not of your religious persuasion. (Loud cheers from the pro-abortionists.)

Libertarian: I never thought that I would find myself in agreement with an atheist. How can we Americans of various religions live in peace, if each tries to impose religious beliefs on all the rest of us by struggling to get laws changed through aggressive tactics including killings? With all due respect, Reverend, you and yours are destroying the American

	experiment which strains to accommodate almost 300 million people of various religions to live in harmony. No country half our size has ever succeeded in this experiment and you are aborting the fledging experiment. No pun intended.
Pro-abortionists:	Right on! You tell him Libby.
Policeman:	The neighbors are complaining that your clamoring is disturbing their siesta. You got five minutes to summarize your shouting match and depart. The neighbors have a right to their siesta. I asked the town recorder to summarize for you.
Town recorder:	We learned some medical facts. We were reminded of the law allowing abortion up to three months. Our moral discussion led us to the distinction between potential and actual human life, plus the woman's right to privacy. We are implored to give America a chance for peace by not imposing one religious view on everyone. Finally, the crucial puzzle is that we don't know when human life begins.
Both groups:	We will continue this dispute at Joe's Bar around the corner next week at 3 P. M. sharp and don't forget your placards.

Curtain falls. No applause, please.

Class Debate

The anti-abortionists defend the position that even though at conception there is no actual human life but only potential human life, it would still be murder to abort.

The pro-abortionists defend the position that at least at conception there is no actual human life and a woman may abort from the time of conception till the time of actual human life whenever that may be.

Discussion

1. What's the difference between a moral and a legal abortion?

2. Why would anti-abortionists call a moral abortion an oxymoron?

3. Explain why you agree or disagree with the philosopher's claim: "The precise issue of the abortion debate should be when does human life begin?"

4. Explain what the doctor means when he says, "I cannot answer that question."

5. Explain the difference between actual and potential human life.

6. Explain what the pregnant woman means by her right to privacy?

7. Is she or is she not entitled to her right of privacy?

8. Would an anti-abortionist be morally justified to kill a doctor who performs abortions?

9. Would an anti-abortionist be morally justified to threaten to kill a nurse who works for a doctor who performs abortions?

10. Comment on the epigraph.

CHAPTER 29

Do Animals Have Rights?

"All animals are equal, but some animals are more equal than others."

George Orwell

Letters to the Editor

Dear Editor:

Before your readers bury their heads in the following letters about animal rights I want to define a right according to Webster's Dictionary: "Something to which one has a just claim: as the power or privilege to which one is justly entitled as upon principles of morality, religion, law or custom . . ." In other words, rights refer to claims made by competent human beings. Take it from here editor.

Lori Sniff, librarian (1)

Dear Editor:

There are barrels of opinions on animal rights. I salute the most liberal views. (2) First, we hold that it's morally acceptable to kill animals for food, clothing, jewelry, and even for sport recreation like hunting. Second, we also maintain it morally acceptable to keep animals for domestic use as pets, for circus entertainment, and for education in zoos. Third, and most important, in all the above-mentioned morally permissible situations, we firmly teach the avoidance of unnecessary physical pain caused through injury and neglect.

Sid Freely, City Zoo President

Dear Editor:

Since the writer above gave no justification for his assertions, I'll do the same. I agree only with the third plank of his platform. I represent the view of many vegetarians. First, it's morally unacceptable to kill animals except for self-defense. Consequently, we abstain from meat because it's tainted with killing. Second, we oppose domestication of wild animals because it confines them in an unnatural environment instead of the wilderness, their natural habitat.

Stanley Plant, Secretary, Veg Trucking Union

Dear Editor:

We psychologists, scientists, especially medical researchers and veterinarians, are often compelled to experiment on animals. However, we first ask ourselves whether the experiment is necessary, useful or fun. We don't experiment for fun. We debate at times whether an experiment would offer us useful knowledge. We share the opinion that it would be moral if the experiment were necessary.

Before we perform our necessary experiments we try to substitute computer simulations, non-invasive scanning, in vitro research, and we properly anesthetize these animals. (3) Since we feel morally justified in experimenting on lower forms of animal life in order to cure diseases and ills of higher forms of animal life, with greater reason we feel morally justified in experimenting on animal life in order to cure diseases and ills of human life. Besides, we wrangle among ourselves as to whether some experiments are necessary to perform on live animals in order to teach our students.

Dr. Sue Scalp, Lab. Supervisor

Dear Editor:

A traditional philosopher's view on animal rights asserts that although animals have no rights per se it does not follow that we humans may treat them with cruelty. As human beings we remain obligated to treat them kindly for the simple humane reason that animals experience feelings and therefore they can suffer agonizing pain all along the scale from the psychological to the physical.

Before you assign this letter to the wastebasket let me explain what I mean when I assert that animals have no rights. Moral beings have rights because they have responsibilities and duties. No responsibilities no rights. Animals cannot be blamed for actions and marched into court. Instead, the owners of the killing pit bulldogs are dragged into court and dogs themselves often go scot-free.

Now I know that there are philosophers who will make your head spin by creatively arguing how animals have moral rights just as humans do. They may write to you if they so desire.

George Cratic, Past President of The United Society of Socrates

Dear Editor:

I'm shooting in favor of the opinion that hunting is ethical. (4) My first ethical shot says that one is ethically allowed to hunt for food. My second volley claims that some animals, e.g., deer, ought to be shot because at times they ruin lands, spread disease to humans, and overpopulate. Our ethical code demands respect for animals by not being cruel to them and by not killing to acquire a reputation.

Phil Shootie, Manager of the Wild West Lodge

Dear Editor:

I opt to fire back and defend the position that hunting is unethical. Hunters don't hunt for food. They don't kill sick animals but they shoot healthy ones to show off. Trapping is cruel and unnecessary to control overpopulation. Besides, the hunters' code of ethics is a paper tiger.

Josephine Snipe, Manager of the Anti-Hunters' Lodge

Dear Editor:

Of all those who wrote you letters not one of them mentioned the Bible. As a Christian I consult my Bible whenever I'm confronted with a problem. I found a text, which I interpret to mean that animals have rights. It's the story of creation where God says of the newly created couple, Adam and Eve: "Let them have dominion over the fish of the sea, and over the birds of the air, and over the cattle, and over all the earth, and over every creeping thing that creeps upon the earth," (Genesis 1:26). (5) There are other relevant texts.

Felix Giddys, Publisher

Dear Editor:

I would like to reply to the happy Christian publisher. He quoted Genesis to prove that animals have rights. On the contrary, I argue that the text declares that man has rights over the animals. God has given dominion (6) over the animals to the newly created couple.

My more significant reply to the publisher is to recall a basic rule of biblical interpretation: one may not quote a biblical text as proof for or against a modern problem unless that biblical text happens to be talking about that precise modern problem. There is nothing in the Genesis text that proves that the author was thinking of our modern controversy.

Joe Click, Trouble-Shooter for Biblical Scholars Anonymous

Dear Editor:

I am a Hindu. With all due respect, a practicing Hindu is offended by all the letters to the editor. We Hindus respect animals. We won't even begin to discuss such an indecent question about the rights of animals. Why not? Because our religion teaches that we must cultivate the virtue of compassion for all sentient beings (beings with feeling) including animals (and not only cows).

Krishna Ram, Guardian of the local Ashram

Discussion

1. Do you agree with the most important moral argument in the animal rights

issue, i.e., animals per se have no rights but humans are obligated to treat them with respect?

2. There are people who respect animals more than they respect humans. Comment.

3. Contrast an ethical with an unethical procedure of dissecting an animal in the biology lab.

4. Present four examples of cruelty to animals that you witnessed in real life, the movies, and the news.

5. Would you surrender the money spent on your pet animal during the last two months in order to save a child from starvation in Africa? If so, would your action be done out of charity (out of generosity) or out of justice (out of a sense of it being owed to the children)?

6. Do you agree or disagree with the vegetarian's opposition to domesticate wild animals? (See the third letter above.)

7. Do you approve or disapprove of a friend who tortures animals for fun only on holidays?

8. Do you know anyone who hunts ethically? Unethically? One who never thinks of either?

9. Were you aware of the Hindu teaching as expressed in the last letter above? Comment.

10. Begin to reread the ten letters to the editor. As soon as you locate a moral

question, which in your opinion was never answered, discuss it with your peers.

11. Comment on the epigraph.

CHAPTER 30

What's All This Weeping About Euthanasia?

"Mark how fleeting and paltry is the estate of man . . . yesterday in embryo, tomorrow . . . ashes."

Marcus Aurelius, Roman Emperor

A One Act Play

Scene: A street outside a courthouse

Time: 1990s

Occasion: The trial of Dr. Kevorkian

Cast of characters: Passersby

Beautician:	Who's on trial today?
Local reporter:	Dr. Kevorkian
Howard:	Who's he?
Newspaper boy:	He's a Michigan doctor who assists dying people to end their lives. He rejects all legal warnings and deliberately wants to be tried in a court of law.
Flight attendant:	Dr. Kevorkian lives in the wrong country. If he were in the Netherlands there wouldn't be any trial because it's legally allowed there.

Julia: By the way, Beth, do you know what euthanasia means? That's what a lot of people are yelling about.

Beth: I always thought euthanasia was a girl's name till I opened Webster's Dictionary last night. Mr. Webster writes that euthanasia comes from two Greek words meaning "good and easy death…the act…of painlessly putting to death persons suffering from incurable conditions or diseases." I memorized it because of our vocabulary test today.

Julia: Mr. Philosopher, what's the moral problem about euthanasia and in one intelligible sentence?

Philosopher: Here's the moral problem. When people are so physically ill that there is no hope of recovery, may they end their lives with or without help of others?

Minister, Rabbi, Priest: No, because God gave life and only God can take it away.

Philosopher: You just heard the religious view about euthanasia. Here is the non-religious or secular view. First, parents, not God, give life. Therefore, the sick person has the right of self-determination. If a human being has a right to do as he pleases with his own possessions, what can be a more personal possession than his own body? Second, all humans have a right to be free from unreasonable suffering. Third, no religious belief should be imposed on all Americans.

Carpenter: What's the rule that a sufferer uses to justify taking his own life?

Philosopher: The rule of the quality of life, which will differ with each person. What is a quality of life for one person may not suit another.

Moviegoer: I once saw a video illustrating the quality of life argument, "Whose Life is it Anyway?" The sculptor (played by Richard Dreyfuss) survives an auto accident but is paralyzed from the neck down. Since he could no longer sculpt he asked to die. His girlfriend, doctors, nurses all tried to persuade him to choose another lifestyle because his mind was clear. He refused. He pleaded that his quality of life was that of a sculptor and nothing else. He begged for death and won his case in court.

Philosopher: Did the sculptor make a moral or immoral choice?

Teacher: I'll show that video to my students and ask that question.

Exercises

1. What do you think of Dr. Kevorkian's crusade? Does he deserve jail or not and why?

2. Should America follow the example of the Netherlands where doctor assisted euthanasia is legal?

3. What's your opinion about Japanese children committing hari-kari because of poor grades in school?

4. In your opinion how does euthanasia differ from suicide?

5. The video mentioned above, "Whose Life is it Anyway?" is based on a play with the same name by Brian Clark, (New York : Dodd, Mead & Co., 1979). Select two passages from either the video or the play wherein the sculptor most clearly expresses his wish to die based on his argument of the quality of life as a sculptor.

6. Comment on the epigraph.

EPILOGUE

What's The Biggest Defect Of The Human Race?

"What wisdom can you find that is greater than kindness?"

J. J. Rousseau

Invitation to a Discussion

The greatest defect of the human race was, is, and will be, how to get along in peace with one another as individuals and as nations.

A flashback to the birthday of humankind and to its aging down to the present century will exhibit thousands of wars among peoples and billions of crimes among individuals — murders, thefts, injustices of every color.

We will brush aside from consideration all the calamities of Mother Nature — storms, floods, earthquakes, etc. They alone would cause enough human grief.

If we were enthroned on a cloud, gazing down on the highway of human history, would we not conclude that the human race lavished more effort on the nurturing of reason than on how to get along — than on how to control our negative emotions or feelings?

To whom would you point the finger of accusation for this lopsided education of the human species? The culprits comprise all classes of society including the philosophers from Aristotle all the way down to his intellectual heirs twirling on the philosophical chairs of academia today. The stoic philosophers from 300 B. C. to A. D. 300 may take a bow as the exception as well as Buddha in the 6th century B. C. They shaped a philosophy that preached the proper role of emotions.

The blame game aside, there is no denying that the most luscious fruits harvested from the tender cultivation of reason are math and science. Largely because of this happy couple we enjoy more human comforts now than ever before in history: medical cures lessen human sufferings and increase life expectancy; the means of travel grow faster and safer; the amount of knowledge continues to explode; the information age, the latest darling of science and technology will far outshine the industrial revolution in the arena of human achievements.

Likewise, no one can deny that parallel with the development of reason through math and science, the emotions developed through literature and the fine arts of painting, music, sculpture, architecture. However, this variety of emotional development did not suffice to tame human feelings resulting in peaceful living.

Finally, it's incontrovertible that history has always been sprinkled with individuals, communities, and even some countries, which may have lived in peace and controlled their negative actions and feelings. However, we are addressing the problem of all humans in all of history.

Let's rush to the town hall to continue this discussion.

Devil's advocate: I object. The greatest defect of the world is overpopulation. If we had fewer people the quality of the environment and the standard of living would improve for everyone.

Philosopher: An intelligent objection. However, to the degree that overpopulation is caused by a lack of self-control, it may rate as the second greatest defect. Besides, even in a smaller population, control of negative feelings would remain the number one defect, as in past history when the world population was less than now.

Rabbi: Doesn't traditional wisdom teach that pride and greed are the roots of all evil?

Philosopher: Pride and greed are emotions or feelings. They should be controlled.

Pastor: I'll launch a different objection against the claim that humans have not been sufficiently concerned with the control of negative feelings. Have not world religions taught self-mastery and love of neighbor through the centuries? For example, do unto others as you want them to do to you.

Cynic: What happened to love of neighbor throughout all the burning wars of religions including those today among Christians, Jews-Muslims, Hindus- Muslims?

Skeptic: That remark by my sister fires up the question whether religions did more harm than good in the history of humans.

Philosopher: Nobody can solve that riddle adequately because it's too complex. Religions caused enormous good and countless unintended evils. In final analysis, religions have failed to tame human beings' evil feelings as on-going religious wars testify. However, my question refers to the entire world, religious and secular, in which reason was developed and given more importance than the control of feelings for peaceful living. The world did not emphasize the education of emotional control, with the purpose of acquiring the art of getting along or the art of compromise. This art was a hit and miss project. If families, schools, nations all over the world had historically taught children how to treat others kindly, peace would have reigned supreme. The world as a whole did not and does not value the art of how to get along with others, as much as the science of how to develop the intellect.

Policeman: So what's the remedy? How do we train citizens throughout the world to live peacefully with their neighbors?

Counselor: We might begin by shedding the false motto of "Let it all hang out." If this motto means express your feelings physically even if you have to disfigure somebody's face, then it's a savage slogan. What if somebody's face is your own? But if the motto means, let it all hang out by expressing your feelings verbally, it would be a healthy battle cry.

Psychologist: We can't always squelch the feeling itself. For example, if every time a thug catches sight of an African American or an Asian American he might feel like punching him. As I have often said, the important problem is not that the feeling comes alive but what do you do with that feeling? If you surrender to it, you're a bully. If you conquer it, you're a hero. To vent your anger invites anger in return. To control your anger invites respect. Instead of damaging someone's face, strike out at a punching bag. Also, sports are legitimate outlets for energy seething under feelings of anger, hate, prejudice. To conquer oneself is a greater achievement than to conquer Mount Everest. (Applause)

Student: I still don't understand how we develop self-mastery, self-control.

Counselor: Simple. Just practice doing things contrary to your negative feelings. Don't tease your sister when you know it angers her. Carry out the garbage without father reminding you. Pick up your clothes after yourself in your room without mother nagging you. The more you act against your selfish feelings the more you become the captain of your body. Then one fine day when a juicy temptation comes smiling at you like sex and drugs, you'll possess the practiced habit of saying no. If throughout your life you cave in to selfish petty feelings, you'll roll over like a log the day you meet a giant temptation. I would highly recommend that you attend my conflict resolution classes.

Cynic: Even if a one-horse town like ours learned how to live in peace that would not solve the colossal enigma of how to get the whole world to live in peace.

Advertising agent: The trick to change the world's mentality about any idea is to stage a world convention. For instance, advertise an international convention to be held in Tokyo since the Japanese already have an enviable reputation for settling disputes without lawyers. Advertise that the focus will be how to live in peace. What will happen? This. The lectures will ventilate many ideas. Some will be brilliantly practical, many will be semi-practical, and a few will be ludicrous. The convention will have at least raised the level of the world's consciousness to the need of getting along.

Exercises

1. Write a three-page essay on what you think is humankind's greatest defect.

2. Compare the thesis above — that man's greatest problem is uncontrolled negative feelings — with the sarcasm that man's greatest problem is other people.

3. Discuss what kind of a world we would be living in today if humankind throughout history would have emphasized the control of evil feelings instead of the development of reason/intellect?

4. The World Peace Foundation (1) was founded in 1910 to encourage international peace and cooperation. It publishes an annual report on all the

countries where it tried to solve conflicts peacefully. Do you see any connection between the aim of this Foundation and the biggest defect discussed above?

5. Comment on the epigraph.

APPENDICES, NOTES AND BIBLIOGRAPHY

APPENDIX A

One Liner Meditations On Seneca's Ethical Tunes

A Bio of Seneca (4? B. C.-A .D. 65)

Lucius Annaeus Seneca, the Roman stoic philosopher, statesman, dramatist, was born in Cordoba, Spain to wealthy Italian immigrants. His brother was the biblical Gallio mentioned in Acts 18:12 (1) before whose court the Jews dragged St. Paul for breaking the law.

Seneca studied in Rome where he attained fame as a writer and orator. Accused of adultery with the emperor's sister, Julia, Seneca was exiled to the island of Corsica for about eight years. On his return from exile to Rome he was appointed the tutor of the 11-year-old Nero. Seneca increased his political influence and material wealth. Meanwhile, as Nero, now emperor, engineered a chain of murders, he cast a shadow of guilt by association over his ministers of state, including Seneca. For this reason Seneca retired to one of his villas.

Nevertheless, he was implicated in a conspiracy with Piso to assassinate Nero who therefore ordered Seneca to commit suicide. He drank the hemlock in imitation of Socrates' noble suicide — also unjustly condemned. Seneca's wife freely chose to accompany him and die in like manner.

As a stoic philosopher Seneca taught lofty, practical morals in his numerous essays and letters. (See a resume of stoic teachings in chap. 18.) His writings overflow with insights on the tranquility of life, the brevity of life, happiness, wisdom, clemency, providence. It may surprise the moguls of Hollywood that Seneca protested vehemently against the cruelty of gladiator spectacles and the institution of slavery. His letter 47 blisters with a stronger repudiation of slavery than any Old Testament or New Testament writing, including the epistles of St. Paul.

Seneca's teachings have been neglected in the English-speaking world, by academicians, publishers, and therefore the general reader. (The amount of ink splurged on his character flaw, that he praised poverty as he sat in the lap of luxury, could have been more justly and profitably spent on popularizing his ethical doctrine.) In Latin textbooks the favorites of the golden age of Latin literature are Caesar, Cicero, Virgil. Seneca unfortunately wrote his scrolls in the silver age of Latin literature. His Latin may be cast in silver but his thoughts are cast in gold.

Seneca's writings were so highly esteemed in Christian Europe that in the third century St. Jerome considered the apocryphal letters between Seneca and St. Paul, his contemporary, to have been genuine. (2) Moreover, Seneca's tomes contain as many as 38 parallels or similarities to the Bible. (3) A cursory reading suffices to prove why Seneca was so popular with the Christians of the Middle Ages.

Not only was Seneca passed over in philosophical and classical studies but also in English literature. His nine tragedies, probably intended for dramatic readings, closet dramas, rather than stage productions, influenced the incomparable Shakespeare himself, an unforgivable secret in textbooks of English literature.

Seneca's essays and letters teem with ethical ideas and ideals still relevant today.

They are expressed in common "silver" language, which makes for easy reading by anyone from high school on up.

The 20 sayings below, selected from his random essays and letters, are offered to high schoolers from a cornucopia of other gems of equal value. The translations are my own.

1. Whenever I look back at my spoken words, I begrudge the mutes.
2. Mother Nature commands me to do good to others.
3. Don't follow the crowd.
4. It's not worth possessing something valuable unless you can share it with a friend.
5. Differentiate between necessities and superfluities.
6. Never permit your desires to roam beyond the threshold of the wholesome.
7. Each person molds his own character. Chance molds his occupation.
8. It is most idiotic to judge a person either by his clothes or by his social standing.
9. A person is not free if his body is his master.
10. I'll forgive before I'm asked.
11. I shall do nothing to please men: I shall do everything to please my conscience.
12. Fidelity is a most sacred moral goodness of the human heart, incorruptible by bribes.

13. Fire tests gold: calamity tests the strong.

14. They who permit themselves to be hurt by insults need a dose of self-confidence.

15. Don't suffer until a misfortune strikes or you'll suffer more.

16. Your life will seem brief if you measure it by hollow pleasures.

17. Where virtues reside, there will unity dwell; where vices reside, there will disunity dwell.

18. Who was ever bold enough to tell himself the truth?

19. True happiness is rooted in virtue.

20. It is not easy to travel from earth to the stars.

APPENDIX B

Chapters According To Their Literary Forms

Chap. 1	Lecture	Chap. 16	Debate
Chap. 2	Lecture	Chap. 17	Imaginary Trialogue
Chap. 3	Conversation and Diagram	Chap. 18	Séance and A Happy Test
Chap. 4	Imaginary Dialogue	Chap. 19	Lecture
Chap. 5	Conversation	Chap. 20	Vaudeville Show
Chap. 6	Conversation	Chap. 21	Meeting and An Ethics Test
Chap. 7	Interview	Chap. 22	Chart
Chap. 8	Conversation	Chap. 23	Diagram
Chap. 9	Conversation	Chap. 24	Book Summary and Roundtable
Chap. 10	Conversation and a Novel	Chap. 25	Town Meeting
Chap. 11	Conversation	Chap. 26	Private Conversation
Chap. 12	Conversation	Chap. 27	Gay Parade
Chap. 13	Lecture	Chap. 28	One Act Play
Chap. 14	Book Review	Chap. 29	Letters To The Editor
Chap. 15	Imaginary Summit Meeting	Chap. 30	One Act Play

APPENDIX C

Suggested Teachers For Friendly Chapters

Teacher	Chapters
Science	1, 2, 4, 9, 10
Biology	28, 29, 30
English	3, 5, 6, 7, 25
Social Science	12, 13, 16, 17
History	14, 15
Physical Ed.	18, 20, 24
Counselor/Chaplain	8, 11, 19, 21, 22, 23, 26, 27

(or to be selected by or distributed among teachers)

APPENDIX D

How To Use This Book And An Explanation Of The Chapter Arrangement In The Table Of Contents

1. A high school team teaching group will find a suggested distribution of chapters in Appendix C.

2. Members of a study club who never studied philosophy may follow the chapters consecutively and consult the questions at the end of each chapter or generate their own.

3. An individual adult reader who never studied philosophy may want to read the chapters consecutively with the appended questions and bibliography.

4. High school teachers: Chapters 1–3 (Introduction) teach how to differentiate issues of science, philosophy, and religion, and how to argue from the Bible of a religion.

Note: Assuming that the majority of American high school students are probably Christian, I stressed throughout the book the need of tolerance of others' views. Moreover, since these same Christians probably never studied the Bible in a scholarly manner, I included in chapter 3 an explanation of the formation of the Bible plus some rules of interpretation. Finally, to parry the objection that philosophy weakens a Christian's faith, please see "the false fear of philosophy" in the preface.

The teacher may now begin to effect the most fundamental purpose of the book — to develop critical/logical thinking — by continually alerting students in discussions to five essentials (to be augmented and amplified in subsequent chapters): defining terms, focusing on the issue, using reason not feelings, avoiding fallacies, and asking for evidence/proof (to counteract gullibility). Teachers must encourage students to express their own thought-out reasons for or against the author's answers instead of memorizing them. To the extent that students develop critical/logical thinking, they may consider this course a success.

- Chapter 4 exemplifies the teaching contained in chapters 1 through 3.

- Chapters 5 and 6 Logic-Fallacies: The teacher will alert students, throughout the course, to implement the rules of logic and to avoid fallacies.

- Chapter 7, on the media, may be used here to immediately apply the teaching of the two preceding chapters; or, chapter 7 may be added to the other ethical issues after chapter 23.

- Chapters 8 through 11 offer students more practice in differentiating issues of science, philosophy, and religion as explained in chapters 1 through 3. *Candide* by Voltaire in chapter 10 may serve as a respite, or may be postponed after part two of chapter 11 (Why so much evil?).

- Chapter 12 on government may be omitted if the students studied the problem sufficiently in their civics course.

- Chapters 13 through 17 present warm-up ethical issues in preparation for chapter 21. They may be postponed until after chapter 21.

- Chapters 18 through 20 may serve as a respite at any time during the course.

- Chapter 21 on ethics and chapters 5 and 6 on logic-fallacies form the backbone of the book.

- Chapters 22 and 24 through 30 treat ethical issues. Regarding the choice of the issues see the preface, "Let's be practical." For the importance of tolerance of the views of others, see the preface "ethics." The teacher may now insist more that the students apply the rules of logic and avoid fallacies in addition to applying ethical rules. The teacher must convince the students that the habits of thinking logically and ethically will serve them more profitably in life than the quest for a definite answer to the ethical problems. Most of the time, there are no definite answers.

- Chapter 23 may serve as a mid-term self-examination. The examination will make the students aware of where they stand on the scale of ethical growth as they approach the following ethical issues. However, the teacher may postpone this chapter until the end of the book

- **Epilogue:** What's The Biggest Defect Of The Human Race? Philosophers like to ask the broadest questions of which the human mind is capable. This question seems appropriate here after all the problems of the book have been discussed.

A final note: A scholarly division of the chapters (not a psychological division to hold the students' interest) may begin with the introduction (how to differentiate problems of science, philosophy, and religion) followed by the chapters on logic-fallacies and ethics. The middle of the book would constitute all the ethical issues and the other issues in which the students are expected to apply the logical and ethical rules. Chapter 23 would end the book with a self-examination.

BOOK NOTES

Chapter one

1   The epigraphs do not necessarily refer to the contents of the chapters. Like window dressing, epigraphs welcome readers into the think-boutique.

2   Chapters end with "exercises" (questions, discussions, working out, etc.) Although these exercises relate to their respective chapters, they do not intend to summarize nor review the contents of the chapters. Few exercises actually test whether students understand. The exercises serve as substitutes until students voice their own questions for discussion.

Chapter two

1   For several examples of fraud see David Marks, The Psychology of the Psychic (Amherst, New York: Prometheus Books, 2000, 2nd ed.), pp.123-135.

2   I assume full responsibility for this explanation which I based on A. Flew, "perception," in The Encyclopedia of Philosophy, Collier Macmillan, New York, reprint ed., 1972, Vol. 6, pp. 436-441 and on David Gay Griffith, 'Why Critical Reflection on the Paranormal is so important and so difficult" in Michael F. Stoeber and Hugo A. Meynell, eds., Critical Reflections on the Paranormal (New York: State University of New York Press, 1996), p. 109.

3   All references to Webster's Dictionary and to "dictionary" refer to Webster's Third New International Dictionary of the English Language Unabridged.

Chapter four

1   For a few examples of how scientists were hampered, see J. J. C. Smart, "Religion and Science," in The Encyclopedia of Philosophy, ibid., Vol. 7, p. 158.

Chapter six

1 The epigraph by P. Bayle is quoted, but not verbatim, from Frederick Copelston, A History Of Philosophy (New York: Doubleday, 1964, pb.), Vol. 6, p. 19.

Chapter seven

1 I assume full responsibility for the wording of this insinuating question even though I am inspired by David Archard, "Privacy, The Public Interest and a Prurient Public," Matthew Kieran ed., Media Ethics (New York: Routledge, 1988), pp. xxii-xxiii and chap. 7.

2 This is my interpretation of Philip Paterson and Lee Wilkins, eds., Media Ethics: Issues and Cases (Dubuque, Iowa: William C. Brown, 1994), pp. 203-204.

3 The 13 hints are my own.

4 An outstanding exception is Paul Krugman, an economist at Princeton University and a columnist for The New York Times. "We don't have censorship in this country; it's still possible to find different points of view. But we do have a system in which the major media have strong incentives to present the news in a way that pleases the party in power and no incentives not to," (Arizona Daily Star, May 14, 2003, p. B7; email: krugman@nytimes.com).

Chapter eleven

1 The quote is from John Bartlett, Familiar Quotations (Boston: Little Brown and Company, 1968, 14th ed.), p. 436.

2 My translation from the French of Pascal's Pensees as quoted in Bartlett, ibid., p. 363, note 5.

Chapter twelve

1   An Asian Statesman is based on Great Decisions (New York: Foreign Policy Association, 1995), pp. 86-87.

2   Atlantic Journal and Constitution, 29 September, 2002, "The President's real goal in Iraq," Jay Bookman. See globalresearch.ca and also The Project for the New American Century,

http: //www.newamericancentury.org/aboutpnac.htm

3   California Educator, May, 1999, p. 22.

Chapter thirteen

1   These conditions are found in various books on ethics. They vary as to number, order, formulation, examples, explanations. For an in-depth discussion see Elliot M. Zashin, Civil Disobedience and Democracy (New York: The Free Press, 1972), pp.110-119 and references. For an updated, practical roundup see James Tracy, ed., The Civil Disobedience Handbook (San Francisco, California: Manio Press, 2002, pb.), 94 pages.

2   A tendency to respond to problems by civil disobedience may be balanced by checking http://www.civiced.org/civitasexec.html which offers a plan of study in cooperation with the National Council for the Social Studies in Washington, D. C.

Chapter fourteen

1   All the following page indications refer to Martha C. Nussbaum, For Love of Country: Debating the Limits of Patriotism (Boston: Beacon Press, 1996.)

2   Tagore, Rabindranath, The home and the World (London: Macmillan and Co., 1919.) This novel is also a movie with the same name produced by

Satyajit Ray. Tagore's university, whose main focus is on cosmopolitanism, is situated in Santiniketan near Calcutta, India.

3   For a detailed explanation of these remarks and for some historical facts not mentioned in history textbooks, see Gore Vidal, Perpetual War for Perpetual Peace: How We Got To Be So Hated (New York: Thunder's Mouth Press/Nation Books, 2002) and Dreaming War: Blood For Oil And Cheney-Bush Junta (New York: Thunder's Mouth Press/Nation Books, 2002.)

Chapter fifteen

1   "Canossa, village in northern Italy where Emperor Henry IV made a humble submission to Pope Gregory VII in 1077: a place or occasion of submission, humiliation, or penance — often used with 'go to' (he went to his Canossa when he reversed his policy)," (Webster's Dictionary).

2   For this clear example and especially for the lucid explanation of the two interpretations I am indebted to Stephen V. Monsma, "Where Church and State Intersect," in David P. Gushee, ed., Christians and Politics Beyond The Culture Wars (Grand Rapids, Michigan: 2002), chap. 13. I assume complete responsibility for statements made.

3   For an article about this partiality see Ken Silverstein and Michael Scherer, "Born Again Zionists" in Mother Jones, October, 2002, pp.56-61.

4   The Last three exemptions and rights are listed but not explained by Thomas Robbins and Roland Robertson, eds., Church State Relations (New Brunswick, N.J.: Transaction Books, 1987), p. 146.

5,6,7   See Church State Relations, ibid., pp.138, 139, 143 respectively.

8   Encyclopedia of American Religions, 5th ed., 1996, p. 16.

Chapter seventeen

1   This enigmatic saying is quoted from Robert G. Ingersoll, The Works of Robert G. Ingersoll (New York: The Ingersoll League, 1929), Vol. II, p.315.

2   These two theories of punishment are explained in many textbooks of philosophy 101, e.g., Joel Feinberg, ed., Reason and Responsibility (Wadsworth: Belmont, California, 7th ed.), chap. 4. I am partial to John Hospers, Human Conduct: An Introduction To The Problems of Ethics (New York: Harcourt, Brace & World, 1961), pp.451-467.

3   The reference for these four objections if any exists is unknown to the author.

Chapter twenty

1   For these three reasons which are explained more philosophically and to which I am indebted see The Encyclopedia of Philosophy, ibid., s.v. "Humor," by D. H. Monroe, Vol. 4, pp.90-93.

2   The Oxford Dictionary of Quotations, 2nd ed., p. 2, #32.

3   The Arizona Daily Star, Beth Francis, 3/14/2001, p. E 1.

Chapter twenty-one

1   The three yardsticks are adapted from and more thoroughly explained by Manuel Velasquez, Business Ethics (New Jersey: Prentice Hall, 3rd ed., 1992), pp. 57-106, passim. I assume complete responsibility for all statements.

2   The four types of teachers' answers are adapted from and extensively explained by Katherine G. Simon, Moral Questions in The Classroom (New Haven, Conn.: Yale University Press, 2001), chap. 7, "Whose Values Will

Get Taught? The Challenge of Pluralism." I assume complete responsibility for all statements.

Chapter twenty-two

1   This chapter is based on Sissela Bok, Lying: Moral Choice in Public Life (New York: Vintage Book, Random House, 1957, pb.). Bok's masterpiece is the most comprehensive, lucid, and well-balanced treatment on the subject. I assume complete responsibility for all statements.

Chapter twenty-three

1   I assume full responsibility of this summary based on Lawrence Kohlberg, "Moral Stages of Moralization: The Cognitive Development Approach," in Thomas Likona, ed., Moral Development and Behavior: Theory, Research, and Social Issues (New York: Holt Reinhart And Winston, 1976), pp. 31-53.

Chapter twenty-four

1   Because Dostoyevsky conquered his addiction to gambling, these words taken from the last page of his novel, The Gambler, may be interpreted as autobiographical.

2   For the list of ten styles of gambling I am indebted to Gerda Reith, The Age of Chance: Gambling in Western Culture (New York: Routledge, 1999), pp. 58-127, passim.

3   For this question and for whether gambling profits local-state economies, Native American gambling, the biblical question, I am indebted to Charles P. Cozic and Paul A. Winters, eds., Gambling (San Diego, California: Greenhaven Press, 1955.) These and other questions are treated extensively and scholarly in a yes and no format. I followed the format of the questions besides various ideas passim. I assume complete responsibility for all

statements made in this chapter.

4   The New York Times, Peter Passell, 1/13/1994.

5   James D. Weinland, How To Think Straight (New Jersey: Adams & Co., 1963), p. 45.

Chapter twenty-five

1   See Will Durant, The Mansions Of Philosophy (New York: Garden City Publishing Co., 1929), p. 283. Durant does not bother to indicate a Greek reference for the definition of unity in variety.

2   For a devastating expose of how the educated public is commercially deceived into accepting poor art as great art in painting, read Tom Wolfe, The Painted Word (New York: Farrar, Straus and Giroux, 1975).

Chapter twenty-six

1   The Arizona Daily Star, Ellen Goodman, 6/23/2002, p. B 2.

2   Ibid.

3   Ibid.

Chapter twenty-seven

1   The quote is from The New Oxford Annotated Bible, RSV, (Revised Standard Version). The New English Bible With The Apocrypha (Oxford University Press, 1970) translates "homosexual perversion."

2   See Joseph A. Fitzmyer, The Anchor Bible, Romans (New York: Doubleday, 1992), Vol. 33, p. 288.

Chapter twenty-nine

1   All names and titles of the letter writers are fictitious.

2   I am indebted to Susan N. Terkel and R. Shannon Duval, eds., Encyclopedia of Ethics (New York: Facts on File, Inc., 1999), pp. 9-10. They propose three types of opinions on animal rights.

3   For this stipulation of anesthetizing I am indebted to Walter G. Jeffko, Contemporary Ethical Issues (Amherst, New York: Prometheus Books, 1999), p.205.

4   For this letter and the following letter I am indebted for several general ideas to Tamara L. Roleff and Jennifer A. Hurley, eds., The Rights of Animals (San Diego, California: Greenhaven Press, 1999), Chaps. 3 and 4.

5   RSV, ibid.

6   The literal translation of the Hebrew word, radah, means to rule or to have dominion. The same Hebrew word is used in verse 28. The text (the Hebrew word) and the context in both verses clearly signify that God gave man complete power over animals. It would be a violation of the text and context to stretch the meaning of the Hebrew word to signify guardianship.

Epilogue

1   The Foundation Report, 2000-2001 (Cambridge, Massachusetts: World Peace Foundation, 2002).

Appendix A

1   RSV, ibid.

2   Edgar Hennecke, ed., New Testament Apocrypha (Philadelphia, PA: Westminster Press, 1964), Vol. 2, p.133.

3   John Hurst and Henry Whiting, L. Annaeus Seneca (New York: Harper, 1899), pp. 40-46.

SELECTED BIBLIOGRAPHY

Chapter one

    1   Gaardner, Jostein, Sophie's World. (New York: Farrar Straus and Giroux, 1994.)

        See pp. 106-196 on Mysticism.

    2   Harvey, Andrew, ed. The Essential Mystics: Selections from the World's Great Wisdom Traditions. (New York: HarperCollins, 1996.)

Chapter two

    1   Gardner, Martin, Fads & Fallacies In The Name Of Science. (New York: Dover Publications, 1957.)

        See chap. 25 for numerous, interesting examples of ESP.

    2   Malcom Gladwell, "The Naked Face, Can you read people's thoughts by looking at them?" The New Yorker, 5 August 2002, 38-49.

Chapter three

    1   Durant, Will, The Story of Philosophy: Lives and Opinions of the Greater Philosophers. (New York: Pocket Books, 1971.)

        See pp. xxv-xxix, "On the uses of philosophy" for a concise, easy to read comparison between philosophy and science.

    2   Kenyon, Frederic G., Our Bible and the Ancient Manuscripts. (London: Harper, 1958.)

    3   Minkoff, Harvey, ed. Approaches to the Bible. (Washington, D. C.: Biblical Archaeology Society, 1994.)

        See Vol. I, chap. 16, Old Testament Manuscripts and chap. 17, New Testament Manuscripts, Uncials, Minuscules, Palimpsests. Kenyon's book listed above is old but more readable than Minkoff's.

    4   Duel, Leo, Testaments of Time: The Search for lost manuscripts and records. (New York: Knoff, 1965.)

              Chaps. 13 &14 provide a captivating account of how Tischendorf searched for biblical manuscripts.

Chapter four

    1   Stanley Kramer, Inherit the Wind, (UA/Lomitas), 127 min., video.

              This video on the 1925 Scopes Trial may be followed by a critique and or a debate between creationists and evolutionists.

    2   Lawrence, Jerome and Lee, Robert E., Inherit The Wind. (New York: Bantam Pathfinder Edition, 1956.)

              This play is not intended as a strict historical account of the Scopes Trial. It's theater. The suggestion above about the video may apply here as well.

    3   Films For The Humanities And Sciences, P. 0. Box 2053, Princeton, NJ 08543-2053; Phone 800 257-5126; www.films.com) 45 mm., video, color. "Coping With Scientific And Social Change: Christianity in the 19th and 20th centuries."

              Creation and evolution are among the several topics discussed.

    4   Aubrey, Frank and Thwaites, William, M. eds., Proceedings of the 63rd Annual Meeting of the Pacific Division, American Association For The Advancement Of Science, "Evolutionists Confront Creationists," Vol. I, Part 3, April 30, 1984. Articles are by creationists and evolutionists.

Chapter six

    1   See Sophie's World, ibid., pp. 88-89 for an example of Aristotle's logic.

    2   Thiering, Barry and Castle, Edgar, eds., Some Trust in Chariots: Sixteen views on Erich von Daniken's Chariots of the Gods. (New York: Popular

Library, 1972.)

>Report on three to ten refutations of von Daniken's thesis, that extraterrestrials visited our planet, from Some Trust in Chariots.

3   Shulman, Max, "Love is a Fallacy," in Engle, Morris S., With Good Reason: An Introduction To Informal Fallacies. (New York: St. Martin's Press, 3rd ed., 1986.)

>See pp. 235-245. This is a must read, hilarious and instructive.

4   Films For The Humanities And Sciences, ibid., "Business Ethics: Truth in Advertising," 28 min., video, color.

>How consumers can detect the confusion of hype and half-truths.

Chapter seven

1   Cohen, Elliot, D., ed., Philosophical Issues in Journalism. (New York: Oxford University Press, 1992.)

>Especially helpful are chap. 5, "Political Power and the Media;" chap. 6, "Objectivity and News Reporting;" chap. 8, "Devices of News Slanting in the Print Media," pp. 237-243.

2   Paterson, Philip and Wilkins, Lee, eds., Media Ethics: Issues and Cases. (Dubuque, Iowa: Brown Publishers, 1991.)

>See chap. VII, "The Ethics Of Photo And Video Journalism" and appendix B, Novel Ideas About Ethics, a list of 12 novels involving journalists "who face ethical dilemmas in the… plot" (Steve Weinberg).

3   Films For The Humanities And Sciences, ibid., "Media Rights And Responsibilities," 30 min., video, color.

>Discusses among other topics the role of government and how society can curb media expression.

4   Films For the Humanities And Sciences, ibid., "Media Ethics," 30 min.,

video, color.

> Professionals from Capitol-EMI Records, Mercury Records, NBC, discuss among other topics: "If a CD by a top recording artist has strongly antisocial lyrics, should the record label consider its impact on kids?"

5   Chomsky, Noam, Power and Terror: Post -9/11 Talks and Interviews. (New York: Seven Stories Press, 2003.)

> This internationally known linguist and political activist of M.I.T. is on a mission to give the real news behind the news.

Chapter eight

1   See Sophie's World, ibid., pp. 324-328 on the origin of life and DNA.

2   Films For The Humanities And Sciences, ibid., "Human Consciousness and Computers," 28 min., video, color.

> Experts discourse about the nature of human consciousness and whether computers can be taught to think.

Chapter nine

1   See Sophie's World, ibid., "The Big Bang," pp. 387-394.

Chapter ten

1   Voltaire, Candide, Zadic and Selected Stories, trans., Donald M. Frame. (New York: New American Library, 1961.)

> There are many available and excellent translations of Candide with helpful introductions.

Chapter eleven

1   Pascal, Pascal Pensees, trans. A. J. Krailsheimer. (New York: Penguin Books, 1976.)

> See "The Wager," pp. 149-155. Pascal bet that if you believe in God and found out at the pearly gates that there is a God, you would be

rewarded; if you disbelieve in God and found out that He exists, you might be eternally damned. Therefore the safer wager is to believe in God. Notice that Pascal, a brilliant mathematician argues like a mathematician and not like a philosopher.

2   Films For The Humanities And Sciences, ibid., "The Quest For God, a search for the handprints of God throughout history and the relevance of Christianity," 43 min., video, color.

3   _____, "Lessons From Job: Desperate with Grief,"43 min., video, color.

> This video explores the problem of evil.

Chapter twelve

1   Ravitch, Diane and Thernstrom, Abigail, M., eds., The Democratic Reader. (New York: Harper Perennial, 1992.)

> See "The Four Freedoms," (of speech, of religion, from want, from fear) by Franklin Delano Roosevelt, pp. 182-183. The president delivered this message to congress in 1941. Have you any reflections about these freedoms in light of the aftermath of the Twin Towers disaster of 9/11?

2   Machiavelli, The Prince, trans., Luigi Ricci. (New York: New American Library, 1952.)

> There are many editions of this popular book, which describes what rulers do to gain and hold political power. Especially modern are chaps.17, 19, 21, 23.

3   Films For The Humanities And Sciences, ibid., "Global Capitalism And The Moral Imperative," 30 min., video, color.

Chapter thirteen

1   The Democratic Reader, ibid.

> See "Civil Disobedience" by Henry David Thoreau, pp. 156-158. This American classic attracts debaters.

2 King, Martin Luther, Jr., A Call To Conscience. (New York: Warner Books, 2001.)

> Compare Thoreau's essay with one of Martin Luther King's speeches.

3 Duncan, Ronald, ed., Selected Writings of Mahatma Gandhi. (London: Faber And Faber, n.d.)

> See principally Part III, "The Practice of Satyagraba or civil disobedience . . . a means of national defense" (against England). Gandhi used the weapon of civil disobedience more successfully than any reformer in modern history.

4 Films For The Humanities And Sciences, ibid., "In Search of Thoreau," video.

> Scholars air their views on his writings including civil disobedience.

Chapter fourteen

1 Nussbaum, Martha, C., For Love of Country: Debating the Limits of Patriotism. (Boston: Beacon Press, 1996.)

2 United Nations World Conference on Human Rights (2nd), World Conference on Human Rights: The Vienna Declaration and Programme of Action. (United Nations Publication, June, 1993.)

> For a cosmopolitan tone see especially the opening statement by the U. N. Secretary-General, Boutros-Boutros-Ghali.

Chapter fifteen

1 The New Encyclopedia Britannica, 15th ed.

> See "church and state" for a brief account from the beginning of Christianity to the present. See also "Fundamentalism" for an outline of the movement from its origins to Jerry Falwell.

2 Encyclopedia Americana, International ed., 1997.

> See "church and state" for a brief history.

3   Neuhaus, Richard John, Christian Faith and Public Policy: thinking and acting in the courage of uncertainty. (Minneapolis: Augsburg Publishing House, 1997.)

      A conservative view.

4   Gushee, David P., ed., Christians And Politics Beyond The Culture Wars. (Grand Rapids, Michigan: Baker Books, 2002.)

      A variety of topics are objectively aired by experts in the spirit of ecumenism.

5   Ken Silverstein and Michael Scherer, "Born-Again Zionists: With their apocalyptic beliefs and powerful political connections, evangelical Christians have emerged as a major force in shaping Bush's policy on Israel," Mother Jones, October 2002, 56-61.

Chapter sixteen

1   Encyclopedia Americana, International ed., 1997.

      See "Capital Punishment" for an adequate treatment of its history and types.

2   Williams, Mary E., ed., Capital Punishment. (San Diego, California: Greenhaven Press, 2002.)

      Opposing experts debate whether capital punishment is ethical; whether it's administered fairly; whether it effectively deters crime; whether it should be abolished. See pp. 151-152 for a bibliography of 17 books; see pp. 152-153 for a bibliography of 28 periodicals (of interest is "The Juvenile Death Penalty"); see pp. 154-156 for 12 organizations concerned with issues related to capital punishment.

3   Fine, Gary Alan, Gifted Tongues: High School Debate and Adolescent Culture. (N. J.: Princeton University Press, 2001.)

4   Jamieson, Kathleen Hall and Birdsell, David S., Presidential Debates: The Challenge of Creating An Informed Electorate. (New York: Oxford

University Press, 1988.)

> Worthy of note are chap. 6, "The Problems of Broadcast Debates," and chap. 7, "The Promise of Debates." Note that the last two books mentioned present a less rigorous approach to the rules of debate than the five foregoing rules and a less rigorous example of a debate than that of the death penalty debate above.

Chapter seventeen

1   Fyodor, Dostoyevsky, The House of the Dead. (New York: Dutton, 1967.)

> See pp. 57-60, "Prison Life in Siberia." Although prisoners serve the same amount of time for the same crime, nevertheless they may differ not only in moral guilt but also in mental and physical suffering.

2   Karl Menninger, The Crime of Punishment. (New York: Viking Press, 1968.)

> This renowned Kansas psychiatrist defends the view that therapy is preferable to punishment.

3   Shannon Brownlee et al., "The Place for Vengeance," U. S. News and World Report, June 16, 1997.

4   Grapes, Byran J., ed., Prisons. (San Diego, California: Greenhaven Press, 2000.)

> Specialists write on: Are prisons effective? How should prisons treat inmates? Should prisons be privatized? Should prisons use inmate labor? See pp. 164-165 for 15 books (mainly, Crime and Punishment in America and Jails: Looking to the Future). See p. 165 for 18 periodicals (notably, "Is Locking 'em up the Answer?" and "A model prison"). See pp. 166-169 for 17 organizations concerned with prison issues.

5   Films For The Humanities and Sciences, ibid., "A History Of Punishment: A Philosophical View," 53 min., video, color.

> The video goes from biblical times to the present and includes a discussion on the death penalty.

Chapter eighteen

1   Aristotle, The Basic Works of Aristotle, trans., Richard McKeon. (New York: Random House, 1941.)

> See pp. 1102-1112, especially p. 1107 for Aristotle's ideas on happiness in his own words.

2   Stumpf, Samuel E., Socrates To Sartre: A History of Philosophy. (New York: McGraw-Hill Book Co., 4th ed., 1988.)

> For a sketch of Epicurus' teaching on happiness, see pp. 109-110, 112-113.

3   Arnold, Vernon, Roman Stoicism. (New York: The Humanities Press, 1958.)

> See pp. 64-82 for Zeno's teachings of which happiness forms a small part in these pages.

4   Russell, Bertrand, The Conquest of Happiness. (New York: H. Liveright, 1930.) _____ Bertrand Russell Speaks His Mind. (New York: The World Publishing Co., 1960.)

> See pp. 83-96, "What Is Happiness?" This is a transcript of a television series. His insights are as practical as they are enjoyable.

5   Hudson, Deal W., Happiness and the Limits of Satisfaction. (Lanham, Maryland: Rowman & Littlefield, 1996.)

> See chap. 2, p. 19, "The Case of Anna Karenina." Anna falsely claimed that she was happy and that led to her suicide.

Chapter nineteen

1   Aristotle, ibid., Nichomachean Ethics, pp. 928-1112.

> There are many available editions of this easy to read masterpiece.

2   Rouner, Leroy, S., ed., The Changing Face of Friendship. (Notre Dame, Indiana: University of Notre Dame Press, 1994.)

> See the following interesting chapters: "When Harry and Sally Read the Nichomachean Ethics: Friendship between Men and Women," "An Indian View of Friendship," "Friendship and Enmity among Nations," "Political Friendship," "Confucian Friendship."

3 Stanhope, Philip, Letters To His Son. (London: The Folio Society, 1973.)

> See pp. 46-49, #15, "How to choose Friends." Note his distinction between companion and friend.

Chapter twenty

1 Greig, J. Y. T., The Psychology Of Laughter And Comedy. (New York: Couper Square Publishers, 1969.)

> Of special interest is the appendix: Theories of laughter and comedy: an historical summary from Plato to Max Eastman.

2 Gomez, Angel M. Garcia, The Legend Of The Laughing Philosopher And Its Presence in Spanish Literature (1500-1700). (Cordoba, Spain: Universidad De Cordoba Press, 1984.)

> The laughing Greek philosopher, Democritus, who died ca. 370 B. C., was reputed to have characteristically laughed at life's problems "without mirth."

Chapter twenty-one

1 Ibsen, Henrik, An Enemy of The People, trans., Christopher Hampton. (London: Faber, 1997.)

> This play exemplifies the high price that a citizen must be ready to pay in choosing to act morally: the loss of home and expulsion from town.

2 Borba, Michele, Building Moral Intelligence: The Seven Essential Virtues That Teach Kids To Do The Right Thing. (San Francisco, California: Jossey-Bass, 2001.)

> Each chapter treats a virtue followed by an annotated list of books, magazines, videos, classified according to age groups. An invaluable,

exhaustive bibliography.

3   De Roche, Edward F. and Williams, Mary M., Character Education: A Guide for School Administrators. (Lanham, Maryland: The Scarecrow Press, Inc., 2001.)

> See Character Education Associations, Institutes, Centers, And Networks, pp. 167-171.

Chapter twenty-two

1   Elizabeth Frazer, Jennifer Hornsky, Sabina Lovibond., eds., Ethics: A Feminist Reader. (London: Blackwell, 1992.)

> See the poet, Adrienne Rich, 'Women and Honor: Some Notes on Lying." This chap. 19 features interesting women's lies to men and the reasons why.

2   James, Henry, A London Life: The Patagonia; The Liar; Mrs. Temperly. Plainview, New York: Books for the Libraries Press, 1976.)

> See "The Liar." In your opinion how would you classify, according to the chart of lies, any five lies spoken by the liar, Colonel Capadose?

3   Films For The Humanities And Sciences, ibid., "The Truth About Lying," 21 min., video, color.

> "In a single day most of us lie…25 times." M. Lewis.

4   _____, "The Psychology of Lying," 30 min., video, color.

> ". . . in a steady stream of information and misinformation, the bond of trust between the government and the governed seems frayed to the breaking point. Can a republic die from too many lies? The question has become critical for the future of democracy. As a philosopher, Sissela Bok grapples with hard truths . . . in this program with Bill Moyers," (blurb, Spring, 2002).

Chapter twenty-three

1   See Sophie's World, ibid., pp. 294-297 for a sketch of the Danish philosopher, Kierkegaard's well-know three stages of life: the aesthetic (one lives according to moods); the ethical (one lives according to morals); the religious (one lives according to religion).

2   Barrett, William, Irrational Man: A Study in Existential Philosophy. (New York: A Doubleday Anchor Book, 1962.)

> See pp. 163-170 for an expansion of the three stages of Kierkegaard mentioned above.

3   Encyclopedia Of Ethics, (1999), "Moral Development."

> See pp. 179-180 for different theories on moral development.

4   Howse, M. E., Spiritual Values in Shakespeare. (New York: Abingdon Press, 1995.)

> The author highlights a virtue or vice connected with a play: Indecision (Hamlet), Jealousy (Othello), Ambition (Macbeth), Ingratitude (King Lear), Bad Intention (Richard III), Good Intention (Julius Caesar), Inhumanity (Merchant of Venice), Tragedy of Life (Tempest).

5   See www.philosphyslam.org for annual prizes for National 1-12 student art and writing competition on philosophical topics. The 2003 Kids Philosophy Slam was: What is the Meaning of Life?

Chapter twenty-four

1   Fyodor, Dostoyevsky, trans., Constance Garnett (The Gambler), Great Short Stories of Fyodor Dostoyevsky. (New York: Harper and Row, 1968.)

> See pp. 379-520 for scenes of the aunt gambling feverishly and the gambler himself caught in the same frenzy of non-stop gambling. They are exciting descriptions of how the demon of gambling seizes

its victims.

2 Cozic, Charles P. and Winters, Paul. A., eds., Gambling, (San Diego, California: Greenhaven Press, 1955.)

> See pp. 197-198 for a list of 17 books; pp. 198-199 for a list of 38 articles in periodicals; pp. 200-202 for a list of 13 organizations concerned with problems of gambling. Experts take opposing views about major gambling controversies. Of special interest are: the 1992 Texas Survey of Adolescent Gambling Behavior; State-Run Lotteries and their effects on school-funding; Controlling addiction to gambling; Most States hold off on legalized video gambling decisions; High Stakes; Low sense of values.

3 Baker, Thomas, Britz, Marjie, Jokers Wild: Legalized Gambling in the Twenty-first century. (Westport, CT: Praeger Publishers, 2000.)

> See chaps, 3,4, 5, on the history of gambling in America; chap. 9, "Why People Gamble," chap. 10, "Youth Gambling, College Gambling," Appendix B: Recommendations of the National Gambling Impact Study Commission, pp. 201 -215.

Chapter twenty-five

1 Loth, David Goldsmith, The Erotic In Literature: an historical survey of pornography as delightful as it is indiscreet. (New York: Julian Messner, Inc. 1961.)

> See chap. 3, pornography in the ancient world; chap. 6, pornography becomes a business; chap. 7, the pornography of the Victorians; chap. 11, facts, fancies, and remedies.

2 Films For The Humanities And Sciences, ibid., "Technology and Pornography," 22 min., video, color.

3 Durant, Will, The Mansions Of Philosophy. (New York: Garden City Publishing Co., 1929.)

> See chap. 23, "What Is Beauty?"

4 Routledge Encyclopedia of Philosophy, 19, "Beauty."

Chapter twenty-six

1   Reiss, Ira L., Solving America's Sexual Crises. (Amherst, N. Y.: Prometheus Books, 1997.)

   See chap. 3 which compares America with other countries and chap. 9, "The role of religion in our sexual crises," especially the last paragraph.

2   Bell, Robert R., Premarital Sex in a Changing Society. (New Jersey: Prentice Hall, 1966.)

   See chap. 3, "Premarital Sexual Attitudes."

3   Roleff, Tamara L., ed., Teenage Sexuality: Opposing Viewpoints. (San Diego, California: Greenhaven Press, 2001.)

   See chap. 1, "What Factors Influence Teen Attitudes Toward Sex?" and chap. 4, 'What Should Teens Be Taught about Sex?" Each of the four chapters consists of articles written by knowledgeable notables. A periodical bibliography ends each chapter. The book itself ends with a bibliography of 13 articles from newspapers/magazines and a list of 16 organizations.

Chapter twenty-seven

1   Roleff, Tamara L., ed., Gay Rights. (San Diego, California: Greenhaven Press, 1997.)

   This book presents the pros and cons on most important debates about homosexuality. See p. 182 for a list of 14 books among which are the Case for Same-Sex Marriage and School's Out: The Impact of Gay and Lesbian Issues on American Schools. See p. 183 for a list of 20 periodicals and pp. 184-186 for a list of ten organizations on gay/lesbian questions.

Chapter twenty-eight

1   The New Encyclopedia Britannica, 15th ed.

   See "abortion" for a concise summary of its medical, historical, legal, and moral aspects.

2 Hurley, Jennifer, The Ethics of Abortion. (San Diego, California: Greenhaven Press, 2001.)

>The book presents opposing views by experts on various aspects of abortion. See pp. 81-84 for 15 organizations with their publications and information. See p. 85 for a bibliography of 11 books and pp. 85-86 for 14 articles from periodicals and newspapers.

Chapter twenty-nine

1 Walker, Alice, Banned. (San Francisco, California: aunt lute books, 1996.)

>"Am I Blue?" pp. 31-43, is a charming anecdotal story about a horse which will convince the reader that animals truly have feelings comparable to those of humans.

2 Roleff, Tamara, L., Hurley, Jennifer, A., eds., The Rights of Animals. (San Diego, California: Greenhaven Press, 1999.)

>Elaborate pro and con chapters treat animal rights experimentation, hunting, animal breeding, the entertainment industry. Pp. 213-215 list 12 organizations with brief description of purpose and publications.

3 Magel, Charles R., Key Guide to Information Sources in Animal Rights. (Jefferson, North Carolina: McFarland & Co., 1989.)

>Pp. 235-236 offer a variety of valuable, diversified, annotated catalogues on all aspects of animal rights issues explained by means of films, videocassettes, filmstrips, musical recordings. Pp. 237-238 feature an evaluated catalogue of national and international magazines/journals, which include the topic of vegetarianism. Pp. 239-240 include a list of products not yet tested on animals.

Chapter thirty

1 Walker, Richard, A Right To Die? (Danbury, Connecticut: Franklin Watts, 1997.)

2 Kubler-Ross, Elizabeth, On Death And Dying. (New York: Macmillan,

1969.)

    The author is internationally known for her theory that people go through five stages when they receive the news of imminent death: denial and isolation, anger, bargaining, depression, acceptance.

3   Films For The Humanities And Sciences, ibid., " Calling Dr. Kevorkian: A Date with Dr. Death," 60 min., video, color.

Appendix A

1   Seneca, Seneca Four Dialogues, trans. and ed. C. D.N. Costa. (Warmington, England: Aris & Phillips, 1994.)

    A Latin text faced with a smooth English translation and a commentary in English await the eager reader. The dialogues are: the life, the tranquility of the mind, wisdom, a letter of consolation to his mother.

2   Seneca Dialogues And Letters, trans. and ed. C. D.N. Costa. (New York: Penguin Books, 1997.)

    Four letters and three dialogues (Consolation, Tranquility, Shortness of Life) await the lucky reader.

3   Seneca 17 Letters, trans. and ed. C. D. N. Costa (Warminster, England: Aris & Phillips, 1988.)

    A Latin text with English translation and commentary. In an epistolary style Seneca shares his stoic ideas couched in such subjects as ethical living, happiness, education, love for his wife, musings, hypochondria, old age, death.

4   Essays on Seneca, trans. and ed. Anna Lydia Motto and John R. Clark. (New York: Peter Lang, 1993.)

    Of the scholarly 21 essays two will appeal to the common man: "Seneca on Drunkenness" and "Seneca on Women's Liberation."

5   Further Essays on Seneca, trans., Anna Lydia Motto. (New York: Peter

Lang, 2001.)

Of the 18 essays, the topics of seven may prove interesting to non-scholars: friendship, pleasure, luxury, restlessness, cruelty, vice, culinary satire.

ABOUT THE AUTHOR

Joseph A. Grispino has earned two graduate degrees in theology and biblical studies in Rome, Italy followed by graduate degrees in education from Boston College and social ethics from the University of Southern California. He taught biblical studies at various divinity schools on the East coast. Professor Grispino continued teaching biblical studies on the West coast at California State University, Northridge. While teaching philosophy at various community colleges in the Los Angeles area he moonlighted for several years as a teacher of Latin at a private high school. The idea of writing the present philosophy book originated at this school.

Grispino has authored four books. Two are introductions and annotations on the Old Testament and the New Testament. A third book, The Bible Now, contains an anthology of articles previously published in his newsletter, Current Scripture Notes. The fourth, Foundations of Biblical Spirituality, is a translation of articles, which had previously appeared in various French periodicals.

During the summers, his travels took him to 33 countries. Speaking skills in five languages added zest to his travels.

Professor Grispino retired from Chapman University in California where he taught philosophy. He is a member of the American Philosophical Association.

BOOK INDEX

A

abortion, viii, 108, 119, 178, 201, **212**–17, 270
animal rights, 220, **218**–**24**, 256, 271
Asian statesman, 97, 102, 251
assumption, 43, 44, **42**–**45**, 123, 189
authority, 11, 12, 15, 16, 51, 86, 166, 202, 203

B

beauty, 41, 192, 197, 198, 269
    what's beauty, **197**–**99**
Bible, 22, **15**–**30**, 209, 241, 246, 255, 257, 274
    interpretation, 22, **24**–**27**, 33–35, 38, 222, 246
    original text, 22–27, 189
    three veils, 22
    translation, 22–26

C

Candide by Voltaire, 77, **79**–**82**, 247, 260
capital punishment. *See* death penalty
capitalist, 93, **100**–**101**
church and state, 36, **115**–**20**, 252, 262
civil disobedience, 108, 251, 262
conscience training, 164–66
cosmopolitan, **109**–**13**, 252, 262
cult, **17**

D

death penalty, viii, **123**–**27**, 130, 263, 264
debate rules, 123–24, 127, **128**–**31**, 200, 263
definitions, 39–42
democracy, 61, 63, 93, **95**–**105**, 110, 195, 251, 267
dictatorship, **93**–**94**, 97, 101
Dr. Kevorkian, 226, 228, 272

E

empirical evidence, **4**–**6**, 9, 73–78, 213
ESP, **11**–**14**, 257
    clairvoyance, 11
    precognition, 12
    psychokinesis, 12
    telepathy, 11
ethics, vii, 15, 133, 147, **158**–**67**, 177, 221, 247–54, 256, 259, 267, 274
    an ethical style, 160
    ethics test, 166
    four guidelines, 159
    of journalists, 259
    three yardsticks, 164
euthanasia, 226–28
evil, 57, 58, 71, **83**–**91**, 117, 134, 159, 160, 201, 203, 212, 232, 235, 261
    evil exercises, 90
    Why so much evil?, **88**–**90**, 247

F

fallacies, 49–56, 130
    fallacy of ad baculum *(Latin—to the stick)*, 51
    fallacy of ad hominem *(Latin—to the man)*, 50
    fallacy of appeal to consensus, 54
    fallacy of appeal to false authority, 51
    fallacy of generalization, 50
    fallacy of inconsistency, 52
    fallacy of non sequitur *(Latin—it does not follow)*, 55
    fallacy of post hoc *(Latin—after this)*, 51
    fallacy of small sample, 50
    fallacy of suppressed evidence, 52
    fallacy of two wrongs make a right, 53
friends, three types, 147–53
    good friend, 149
    pleasant friend, 147
    useful friend, 148

G

Galileo, 31–34, 38
gambling, **182**–**90**, 254, 268, 269
    The Gambler by Fyodor Dostoyevsky, 182–83, 268
gay, **206**–**11**, 255
    gay parade, 206–10
    gay/lesbian rights, 165, 270
God, 21, 27, 34, 35, 37, 73, 75, 215, 221, 227, 256, 260
    and mystics, 6
    Chariots of the Gods by Erich von Daniken, 55, 258
    does God exist, **83**–**88**, 261
    supernatural authority, 15

H

happy life, 141–47
    The Happy Test, 145
homosexual. *See* Gay
human race, 33
    biggest defect of, 230–39

I

in principle, 45
infernal contest, 172
    Dante's Divine Comedy, 172
intercourse and conception, 202, **213**

K

knowledge, 3–15
    and ESP, 11–15
    authority, 6
    mystics and intuition, 6
    non-specialists, 6
    philosophers, 5
    reason, 4
    scientific fact, 4
    the five senses, 4
    the kingdom of, 3
    three royal highways to, **3–7**, 9

L

laugh (why people laugh), 153–57, 266
lying, 53, 88, 166, **168–72**, 172, 267
    definition, 168

M

monarchy, 93–94, 101
morals, **19–21**, 88–90, 240, 268
    adolescent sex, 200–204
    six stages of development, viii, 176–81, 254
mystic, 3, 6, 257

N

non-specialist, 3, 6, 15

O

Osama bin Laden, 133–36

P

patriotism, 109–13, 251, 262
    The Home and The World by Rabindranath Tagore, 110
philosopher, ix, 3–7, **15–21**, 35, 41, 54, 55, 75, 76, 78, 83–88, 90, 96, 119, 127, 133, 144, 159, 164, 160–66, 196, 210, 214, 215, 217, 220, 227–33, 240, 261, 266–69

philosophy, false fear of, ix–x, 246
pornography, viii, **192–97**, 269
possible vs. probable, 12, 45
prima facie, 45

R

reason, 3–8, 9, **11–21**, 31, 49, 54, 73, 75, 76, 73–76, 78, 84–87, 124, 136, 214, 219, 235, 246, 253, 259
    unreasonable, 75, 227
    unreasoning, 56
Richter Scale of Truth, 9

S

scientist, 3–8, 12, 15, 31–35, 37, 40, 71–76, 77, 78, 83, 213, 219, 249
Scopes Trial of 1925, 31–38, 258
sect, 17
Seneca, Lucius Annaeus, 3, **240–43**, 256, 272–73
    20 sayings of, 242–43
senses, the five senses, 4
socialist, 41, 93, **99–101**
superstition, 49, 56–59
    20 superstitions, 57–58

T

theologian, ix, **15–21**, 31–35, **73–76**, 78, 83, 86, 88–90
theology, 27, 84, 274
tolerance, viii, 83, 246, 248

U

universe, 3, 7, 32, 35, 69, 74, 75, 73–76, 84, 85
    Was there always a universe?, 73–76
    Will there always be a universe?, 77–79

V

values, 61, 98, 166, 177, 254, 268, 269
    and art, 199
    family values, 98
    four systems teachers use, 165
    religious, 118
    rights, 110
    six core values in democracy, 104
    value judgment, 46

W

Who am I?, 69–72